Studies in European History

Series Editors:	John Breuilly
	Julian Jackson
	Peter Wilson

Jeremy Black	*A Military Revolution? Military Change and European Society, 1550–1800*
T.C.W. Blanning	*The French Revolution: Class War or Culture Clash?* (2nd edn)
John Breuilly	*The Formation of the First German Nation-State, 1800–1871*
Peter Burke	*The Renaissance* (2nd edn)
Markus Cerman	*Villagers and Lords in Eastern Europe, 1300–1800*
Michael L. Dockrill and Michael F. Hopkins	*The Cold War 1945–1991* (2nd edn)
William Doyle	*The Ancien Régime* (2nd edn)
William Doyle	*Jansenism*
Andy Durgan	*The Spanish Civil War*
Geoffrey Ellis	*The Napoleonic Empire* (2nd edn)
Donald A. Filtzer	*The Krushchev Era*
Karin Friedrich	*Bandenburg-Prussia, 1466–1806*
Mary Fulbrook	*Interpretations of the Two Germanies, 1945–1990* (2nd edn)
Graeme Gill	*Stalinism* (2nd edn)
Hugh Gough	*The Terror in the French Revolution* (2nd edn)
Peter Grieder	*The German Democratic Republic*
John Henry	*The Scientific Revolution and the Origins of Modern Science* (3rd edn)
Stefan-Ludwig Hoffmann	*Civil Society, 1750–1914*
Henry Kamen	*Golden Age Spain* (2nd edn)
Richard Mackenney	*The City-State, 1500–1700*
Andrew Porter	*European Imperialism, 1860–1914*
Roy Porter	*The Enlightenment* (2nd edn)
Roger Price	*The Revolutions of 1848*
James Retallack	*Germany in the Age of Kaiser Wilhelm II*
Richard Sakwa	*Communism in Russia*
Geoffrey Scarre and John Callow	*Witchcraft and Magic in 16th- and 17th-Century Europe* (2nd edn)
R.W. Scribner and C. Scott Dixon	*The German Reformation* (2nd edn)
Robert Service	*The Russian Revolution, 1900–1927* (4th edn)
Jeremy Smith	*The Fall of Soviet Communism, 1985–1991*
David Stevenson	*The Outbreak of the First World War*
Peter H. Wilson	*The Holy Roman Empire, 1495–1806* (2nd edn)
Oliver Zimmer	*Nationalism in Europe, 1890–1940*

**Studies in European History
Series Standing Order
ISBN 0–333–79365–X**
(*outside North America only*)

You can receive future titles in this series as they are published by placing a standing order. Please contact your bookseller or, in case of difficulty, write to us at the address below with your name and address, the title of the series and the ISBN quoted above.
Customer Services Department, Macmillan Distribution Ltd
Houndmills, Basingstoke, Hampshire RG21 6XS, England

Villagers and Lords in Eastern Europe, 1300–1800

Markus Cerman

palgrave
macmillan

First published 2012 by
PALGRAVE MACMILLAN

Palgrave Macmillan in the UK is an imprint of Macmillan Publishers Limited, registered in England, company number 785998, of Houndmills, Basingstoke, Hampshire RG21 6XS.

Palgrave Macmillan in the US is a division of St Martin's Press LLC, 175 Fifth Avenue, New York, NY 10010.

Palgrave Macmillan is the global academic imprint of the above companies and has companies and representatives throughout the world.

Palgrave® and Macmillan® are registered trademarks in the United States, the United Kingdom, Europe and other countries.

ISBN 978–0–230–00460–3

This book is printed on paper suitable for recycling and made from fully managed and sustained forest sources. Logging, pulping and manufacturing processes are expected to conform to the environmental regulations of the country of origin.

A catalogue record for this book is available from the British Library.

A catalog record for this book is available from the Library of Congress.

10 9 8 7 6 5 4 3 2 1
21 20 19 18 17 16 15 14 13 12

Printed and bound in China

To Dana.

Contents

Contents

List of Tables

List of Tables

Editors' Preface

The Studies in European History series offers a guide to developments in a field of history that has become increasingly specialised with the sheer volume of new research and literature now produced. Each book has three main objectives. The primary purpose is to offer an informed assessment of opinion on a key episode or theme in European history. Second, each title presents a distinct interpretation and conclusions from someone who is closely involved with current debates in the field. Third, it provides students and teachers with a succinct introduction to the topic, with the essential information necessary to understand it and the literature being discussed. Equipped with an annotated bibliography and other aids to study, each book provides an ideal starting point to explore important events and processes that have shaped Europe's history to the present day.

Books in the series introduce students to historical approaches which in some cases are very new and which, in the normal course of things, would take many years to filter down to text-books. By presenting history's cutting edge, we hope that the series will demonstrate some of the excitement that historians, like scientists, feel as they work on the frontiers of their subject. The series also has an important contribution to make in publicising what historians are doing, and making it accessible to students and scholars in this and related disciplines.

JOHN BREUILLY
JULIAN JACKSON
PETER H. WILSON

Acknowledgements

Peter Wilson originally suggested this book when he kindly asked me whether I was interested in such a project. For this, I am very grateful to him. I would like to thank all the editors of the *Studies in European History* for their invitation to contribute to their series. Peter's experience and generous advice have guided me through the work. He commented on individual draft chapters and, along with his fellow editors and others, on a first version of the whole manuscript. To him and the other commentators I am indebted for many valuable suggestions.

Many of the arguments of this book are results of continual discussions with colleagues in Europe and the USA over the last 17 years. I would like to mention at least those who knew about this book project, commented on draft chapters or in other ways supported the writing process with information and help. I would like to thank Bruce Campbell, Piotr Guzowski, William W. Hagen, Gergely Horváth, Heinrich Kaak, Erich Landsteiner, Axel Lubinski, Eduard Maur and Carsten P. Rasmussen. I first began research on the agrarian history of Eastern Europe in an international research project, 'Social structures in Bohemia', in the 1990s. The continuous contact with its collaborators helped to shape many of the ideas and arguments presented here. For this I would like to thank all the participants. I also would like to acknowledge the comments I received from people at conferences and seminars during which I presented individual sections of the book: the Annual Conference of the British Economic History Society in 2009; the XVth World Economic History Congress in 2009; the research seminar of the Institut für vergleichende Geschichte Europas im Mittelalter at Humboldt University (Berlin) and the research seminar of the Graduate School 'Baltic Borderlands' at the University of

Greifswald in 2010. I am particularly grateful to Michael Borgolte and Michael North for the invitations to Berlin and Greifswald. The Faculty of Historical-Cultural Studies and the Department of Economic and Social History at the University of Vienna granted a leave of absence during the summer term of 2010, for which I am very grateful. I would particularly like to thank Gabriele Dorner, who kindly drew the map. The Warsaw Państwowe wydawnictwo naukowe granted permission to quote two tables (Tables 4.1 and 4.9) from one of its publications, Andrzej Wyczański's *Studia nad folwarkiem szlacheckim w Polsce w latach 1500–1580* (1960). The services of several libraries and the support of their kind staff were essential in completing this work. I wish to thank the libraries of the University of Vienna, Humboldt University and the University of Cambridge, the British Library and the Staatsbibliothek zu Berlin – Preußischer Kulturbesitz.

Every effort has been made to trace copyright holders, but if any have been inadvertently overlooked, the Publishers will be pleased to make the necessary arrangements at the first opportunity.

I owe a very large debt of gratitude to my host institution during my leave, the Institut für vergleichende Geschichte Europas im Mittelalter (Institute for the Comparative History of Medieval Europe) at Humboldt University. I would like to thank particularly Michael Borgolte for making possible and supporting my stay in Berlin, which was an extraordinary privilege and help. I am very grateful to all the members of the Institut for their repeated generous hospitality, constant support and the magnificent working conditions they offered to me as a visiting scholar in 2009 and 2010 (not to mention earlier stays in different contexts). I also wish to thank Linda Auld and I am particularly grateful to Sally Lansdell for her careful work in editing my original manuscript. I feel extremely privileged and I am tremendously grateful to have had the chance to work together with Sonya Barker, Felicity Noble and others at Palgrave Macmillan. Sonya's consistent support, her kind patience and understanding and her advice in literally a thousand things proved invaluable. The most important support for making possible this book and many other works came from Dana Štefanová. Therefore, my biggest debt is to her. It is to Dana that I wish to dedicate this work.

Glossary

cadastre
a tax survey for taxes based on landholding.

demesne farm
lords often directly managed land in seignorial property in demesne farms. These could be smaller – such as two to three times the size of full tenant farms – or large, latifundium-like units. Theoretically, they could be operated in three different ways: directly, with wage labour; with the help of the labour rents of tenants; or by means of a mixed system between these two modes. Demesne farms were part of the demesne economy.

estate
the unit of property holding of a landlord (identical with the notion of a manor used in a medieval context). An estate could consist of a single village or only a part of a village with only a few tenant households, but could be large enough to comprise many villages and towns and a few thousand tenant households. Richer lords and magnates often held more than one estate and administered their properties as a dominium or latifundium. The meaning of estate as a unit of property has to be distinguished from 'Estates' as a political (a limited form of territorial representative assembly) and social (noble and church landlords/dignitaries and free cities) concept in the late medieval and early modern period.

forced labour services	see labour rents.
fullholding/ full tenant farmholding	a tenant farmstead of standard size within each region liable for full rents and services.
hereditary tenure	the predominant form of tenure for tenant farms, smallholdings and cottages. Tenants held permanent usufruct and mostly also full rights of disposal regarding cultivation, inheritance or sale (partly subject to formal seignorial consent).
hide	a measure of landholding widespread in medieval Europe, but also in parts of the early modern period in certain areas of Central and Eastern Europe, to delimit the size of a typical full tenant farmholding. The actual size varied greatly between different regions and territories. Mostly one hide consisted of between 14 and 25 hectares of land, but could be as large as 40 hectares.
labour rents	part of tenants' obligations to their lords, such as to send draught teams or workers on seignorial demesne farms, or to fulfil transport obligations.
latifundium	large-scale property of land. The term usually refers to the rural estate and property organisation in a Mediterranean context, but is sometimes used for the vast property of the richest noble and church landlords in early modern Eastern Europe.
subjection/subject	used as a translation for the legal status of villagers vis-à-vis their lords in a tenurial relationship; that is, based on the land/ holdings villagers received as tenants from their lords. The dominion of lords over tenants was thus based on land lordship, but could be extended to other areas such as powers of legal jurisdiction. Though the status of subjection did not entail personal bondage, the stricter forms that evolved within demesne lordship could restrict certain personal liberties, such as freedom of mobility.

tenant leasehold
used as a translation for the tenurial form of *Laßbesitz*. The lease was formally limited to a number of years or for life, thus tenants held more insecure property rights over their holdings than in hereditary tenure. Practices in this respect varied widely. Usually lords provided the initial investments for such farms and thus retained rights to claim the property.

terrier
a land survey of an estate that lists seignorial properties and rights and includes a survey or 'extent' of all those holding land from the lord, as well as the rents and services they owe.

village headman
used as a translation for the heads of village communities (German *Dorfrichter*, *Schulze*; Czech *rychtař*; Polish *sołtys*) who often held, together with village jurors, the right of lower jurisdiction in regular village court meetings. Often privileged, these positions could be held in a hereditary manner, or heads of villages could be elected by village communities or nominated by lords.

Map 1 East-Central and Eastern Europe towards the end of the seventeenth century
Key: C: Copenhagen
   S: Schleswig
   H: Holstein
   M: Mecklenburg
   WP: Western Pomerania.

1 Understanding Demesne Lordship

[i] Introduction

Historical research has long assumed that in the early modern period rural societies in Western and Eastern Europe evolved along different paths. As a consequence, the notion of a fundamental 'agrarian dualism' between ancien régime Western and Eastern Europe was established, in which the Western model came to represent liberal modernity and progress and the Eastern re-feudalisation and authoritarianism. Many aspects of this conceptualisation overlap with views of a more general 'backwardness' of Eastern European societies and economies since the early modern period. The historical roots of this thinking, which also relate to the 'otherness' of Eastern Europe, are quite deep and complex [53]. However, based on research emerging since the late 1980s, this book will challenge the view of Eastern European rural society as 'backward' and characterised by a poor, suppressed peasantry ('serfs') and their powerful overlords. Revising this image does not only result in a new account of rural economic and social development in Eastern Europe, but also in questioning the idea of an agrarian dualism between Eastern and Western Europe that is well established in past and current historiography.

[ii] The Historiography of Demesne Lordship

The roots of the concept that two different agrarian systems and an agrarian dualism evolved in early modern Western and Eastern Europe can be found in an authoritative study by Georg

Friedrich Knapp. He offered a general theory of what he thought to be a distinct seignorial system emerging in Eastern German territories, which he named 'demesne lordship' (*Gutsherrschaft*). Knapp belonged to a group of social scientists with liberal and social-reformist attitudes and was a member of the famous *Verein für Socialpolitik* (Society for Social Policy). He called his book, in which he concentrated on the historical causes of the precarious social situation of landless farm labourers on the late-nineteenth-century noble farming estates in 'East Elbian' Germany (the eastern part of the German Empire at the time), a 'socio-political history of the rural population' [6, 26, 34, 115; for a summary of research see 22]. According to Knapp, the villagers' situation deteriorated in the early modern period because of the rising power of the Estates vis-à-vis the (weak) princes and the expansion of farming under direct seignorial management, a means by which the nobles were trying to adapt to their new political and economic roles after the end of the Middle Ages. The concept already implicitly suggested that there was a fundamental difference between the East Elbian situation and that in the West, which to some extent anticipated the 'agrarian dualism' used by later historians [18, 22, 54]. This notion of a structural divide was promoted by German-language research after Knapp and in the 1970s and 1980s also entered international debate and macro theories of economic development in early modern Europe [1, 50], work that also referred to influential studies by scholars in Britain and the USA, such as Francis Carsten [104], Hans Rosenberg [141] and Jerome Blum [2], or in Eastern Europe, such as Marian Małowist [32, 33]. In his excellent and stimulating survey of European economic history since the late Middle Ages, Peter Kriedte summarised the position guiding much of the literature to this point by calling the river Elbe the 'most important socio-economic borderline' in Europe [28].

Different theoretical approaches developed a variety of concepts of demesne lordship and the demesne economy. Various schools of thought concentrated on the legal historical aspects or on commercial large-scale farming in direct seignorial management, but all saw the villagers merely as victims of processes determined by powers and institutions beyond their control. It seems that much of Western research after 1945 relied more on the first approach, concentrating on the legal aspects. For instance, it was supported by the West German history of the 'agrarian constitution' until the 1970s, which largely continued a top-down approach concentrating on legal structures and the powers of noble landlords and Estates. The concentration of powers of land lordship and legal and personal lordship rights, which was assumed to characterise the monolithic East Elbian demesne lordship in contrast to Western seignorial regimes, was often seen as giving lords excessive powers over their subjects [22, 30]. Agrarian history in the former people's republics devoted more attention to the characteristics of the rural economy, in particular to the structure of rents and the burdens of forced labour services (*corvée*), as well as to the significance of the commercial demesne economy for seignorial income and its organisation of work and management.

This macro-level approach of categorising the complexity of early modern rural power structures in certain agrarian 'constitutions' that could be clearly separated from each other was scrutinised and criticised, particularly by Eastern European and East German historians and increasingly by West German and US ones, for being ignorant of social practice; unable to explain the regional and local differences that were increasingly becoming visible through a large body of empirical case studies; and exceedingly and wrongly preoccupied with legal structures rather than early modern rural society and economy. Although this shows that the results of research were exchanged and discussed, the Cold War environment and the division of Europe may have prevented the notion of an agrarian dualism being overcome in these decades.

The awareness of territorial and regional variation, as it emerged in Eastern European research, provided the basis for a critique of notions of demesne lordship or a 'second serfdom' understood as a monolithic system and encouraged comparative studies [18, 20, 31, 34, 39, 44, 156]. Research in the German Democratic Republic promoted the idea of differentiating existing models of demesne lordship, which ultimately led to refuting the notion of a fundamental dualism of agrarian structures within Germany [18, 19, 119]. Studies particularly identified distinct paths of development within Eastern Europe for Czechoslovakia [20] and Hungary [155]. Historians in these countries and in Poland never completely shared the original German-language approaches regarding demesne lordship and also used a different terminological inventory to characterise early modern rural societies and economies.

Despite the major achievements of these Eastern European approaches, which added a vast number of detailed empirical studies, villagers themselves still did not appear at centre stage. Though it declared villagers victims of the domination of lords rather than active participants, Eastern European research devoted more attention to the economic, social and legal situation of villagers and their resistance, especially major movements of unrest as forms of class struggle. In this respect, although the role of villagers in shaping the system by means of resistance was acknowledged, the perspective remained one-sided to a certain extent, looking at rural society through the lens of seignorial oppression and victimisation of villagers. While this is a significant shortcoming, the often sweeping dismissal of Marxist scholarship by some of the post-1990 historiography is unjustified and unhelpful. It is one thing to identify the approach's theoretical weaknesses and unanswered questions, but it seems wrong to disregard entirely the results of this extremely relevant research.

Two further interesting and potentially very fruitful avenues for future research have unfortunately remained at the margin of the debate on demesne lordship, because it was largely confined to discussion within rural and agrarian history. First, the importance of forced labour that is often attributed to demesne lordship (see Chapter 2, Section iv) encouraged analytical comparisons between slave labour and demesne lordship and societies with serfdom [3, 24, 27]. While this provides important insights into the economic and social contexts of the two socio-economic forms and the living standards of slaves and serfs, it has also revealed significant differences between them. Even the strictest form of serfdom theoretically granted more rights to villagers than a slave would usually hold, for instance [3, 24].

That lords commanded villagers to supply forced labour rents in the medieval bipartite manor or in early modern East-Central and Eastern Europe also attracted research by economists. To explain this institutional arrangement, economists investigate the potential influence of labour scarcity and low population density, market structure and economies of scale, or agency problems that may increase the profitability of direct management over alternative arrangements [12, 24, 35, 211]. To fully exploit the possibilities offered by these approaches, it is to be hoped that the common basis of rural historians and (historical) economists will broaden and lead to a greater incorporation of insights from agricultural and development economics into European rural history.

4

[iii]   Criticising Demesne Lordship and Agrarian Dualism

Despite the growing unease with the concept of a structural dualism in research of the 1970s and 1980s, the marginalisation of villagers' experiences was finally overcome when theoretical and methodical changes in social and economic history during the 1980s provided the basis for fresh approaches to studying demesne lordship. These provided a basis for considerable new research efforts that turned towards a 'view from the village' [115]. Demesne lordship is now understood as an umbrella term for a range of highly differentiated rural societies and it is acknowledged that they changed significantly over the early modern period [6, 34, 39, 40, 41, 42, 43, 44, 111, 115, 123; see also 18]. This in turn fuelled criticism of the theory of demesne lordship and of the idea of a European agrarian dualism [44, 54]. The concrete manifestation and experience of the system in practice was regarded as a result of everyday negotiation between lords, state authorities and villagers, mixed with the frequent application of force and violence. Instead of imposing a monolithic concept, scholars now emphasise the diversity of early modern rural society in East-Central and Eastern Europe, a characteristic long accepted for other parts of Europe. Following from this, research also began to look systematically for similarities to other seignorial systems in ancien régime Western and Southern Europe. A more widely adopted comparative approach – as practised for example in the 1990s at the Max Planck research group 'Demesne lordship as a social historical phenomenon' at the University of Potsdam [39, 40, 41, 42] or in an international research project on 'Social structures in Bohemia' [69, 72, 73, 81, 85, 87] – is a necessary prerequisite to overcoming notions of an agrarian dualism or a general second serfdom in Eastern Europe [15, 54].

Naturally, these approaches also face considerable resistance among the scholarly public, who would be forced to give up a convenient macro-level model to separate a 'progressive' from an 'other' Europe. What is more, the emerging interpretations were misunderstood as revisionist and as belittling the dramatic effects of what is often still ill conceived as a general personal serfdom in early modern rural East-Central and Eastern Europe. This critique seems inappropriate [111], because not only does it ignore the evidence that has emerged over the past 25 years, it also tends to misunderstand the aims of such studies. Research no longer investigates rural power relations and institutions from the perspective of feudal overlords and their alleged monopoly of power, but instead identifies the scope for action among villagers, their constant insubordination and undermining of the system and the effects on local manifestations of demesne lordship and its institutions. Demesne lordship could certainly be extremely costly and oppressive for villagers, but it is necessary to identify and explain examples in relation to their context, rather than to generalise such conditions over an area as vast as two-thirds of Europe, comprising around 25 per cent of the European population by 1800 and including many regions with intensive commercialisation and successful proto-industrial and industrial development during the eighteenth and nineteenth centuries.

Instead of referring to 'serfdom', specialised studies nowadays usually refer to the seignorial systems with strong lords and weakened villager rights as 'demesne lordship' or related terms, and refer to serfdom only where it was actually imposed. 'Demesne economy' (*Gutswirtschaft*) is used to convey its economic characteristics, with special reference to the large, commercially oriented demesne farms in direct management (see Chapter 2, Sections ii, iii and iv).

In the early modern period, the area covered in this book consisted of a number of states and territories with quite different institutional structures. One group constituted composite states and empires that included different territories with separate constitutions, on which the central authorities had limited but generally growing influence. Such states included Denmark (which controlled southern Sweden until 1658 as well as Schleswig-Holstein), Sweden (which at certain times included Estonia, Livonia, Finland and Western Pomerania), the Habsburg Empire (with the historical Czech Lands and their separate territories as well as the Kingdom of Hungary), the Polish Commonwealth (Poland, Royal Prussia, the Grand Duchy of Lithuania, which included parts of Belorussia, and parts of Ukraine), Russia and parts of the Ottoman Empire. The area also included smaller, independent territories ruled by a prince, such as Mecklenburg, Eastern Pomerania and East Prussia (before being attached to Brandenburg in 1648 and 1618 respectively), and the Electorates of Brandenburg (which also acquired Silesia in 1740) and of Saxony (with Upper Lusatia after 1635). Regional and territorial variation of rural societies within the same territories and states must be expected given their large and composite nature.

[iv]   Sources

The choice of theory determines the research questions and in turn influences the selection of sources. Research on the initial concepts of demesne lordship was biased towards legal historical aspects and top-down perspectives, because they dominated the historical research of the day and the relevant material happened to be most readily available. The emerging territorial state as an agent in rural power relations in the early modern period produced a mass of related evidence. Apart from land ordinances, law codes, so-called territorial police or peasant ordinances and resolutions of diets, numerous other administrative documents remain important sources of information. These include material from state law courts, reports of contemporary committees investigating prevailing conditions, statements of experts, documentation of conflicts between lords or between lords and the state and, in particular, conflicts between lords and villagers. The efforts of early modern states to tax and conscript their subjects resulted in a large number of land surveys and cadastres from the later sixteenth century for almost all the regions covered in this book. These sources have been investigated by detailed quantitative studies from which important information can be derived, such as size of tenant and demesne farms, their equipment and value, the extent of noble, subject, princely or church property and so on.

Usually of much greater importance for the analysis of social relations on the regional or micro level are documents produced by the administration of estates. Thousands of archives of individual noble, princely/royal and institutional estates have been preserved, although, naturally, a great number has been lost over the centuries, particularly from smaller estates. Complete archives are very rare for the sixteenth century and practically non-existent for the period before 1500, but become more frequent in the 1600s and the most detailed material, such as a series of documents over a long stretch of years, is normally available for the eighteenth century. Such documents fall into two groups, if we do not consider personal papers of estate owners. First are sources that relate to seignorial property, the demesne economy and the seignorial household. These include inventories; surveys of property and receipts such as terriers (surveys of property, dues and services) or registers of feudal rents; documents concerning estate administration, including detailed accounting materials (weekly, monthly, annually), annual balances of income and expenditure of individual units such as demesne farms, but also of the financial transactions of the whole estate; and documents covering correspondence and transactions with external institutions or authorities, such as neighbouring estates or the state administration. In the case of princely/royal property and nobles owning more than one estate, such as Czech, Hungarian, Polish or Russian magnates, there usually also existed a central administration on a higher level, to which the officials of the individual estates reported. Secondly, estate archives include a vast array of materials on the relationship between villagers and lords. To these belong court rolls or registers of seignorial and village courts; seignorial and village land transfer registers; probate inventories; official investigations and surveys; documents of conflicts between villagers and lords or among villagers; villagers' petitions; decree books or books of seignorial decisions on villagers' requests or other matters, surveys of the rural population and seignorial instructions regulating social and economic life in the estate.

It is evident that the bulk of the material was produced by the estate administration and that even if it is concerned with administering villagers' affairs, it will be strongly biased towards the seignorial perspective. This is aggravated by the fact that the rise of demesne lordship brought about an extension and professionalisation of estate administration, deliberately intended to strengthen control over villagers. Some types of sources derive directly from such efforts. Only certain groups of documents, such as letters or petitions, potentially originate from villagers and their institutions. Villagers' autobiographical sketches or account books are rare treasures indeed.

Some of the material, such as accounts or cadastres, tax, land or estate surveys, lends itself to predominantly quantitative approaches. With the rise of microhistory, thousands of petitions and court records, formerly only used for purely illustrative purposes, became the centre of analysis. Thanks to such studies and a more cautious approach to the bias inherent in seignorial sources, it has been possible to reconstruct a more balanced picture of everyday life in demesne lordship.

Chapter 2 addresses the problem of defining demesne lordship and the commercial demesne economy and of discussing its meaning in practice. As a key element, it will explain the differences between serfdom and other forms of subjection. Chapter 3 evaluates influential theories explaining the gradual rise of demesne lordship and the establishment of a commercial demesne economy since the later Middle Ages. Chapters 4 and 5 are devoted to the economic sphere: the organisation and results of the commercial demesne economy, as well as the influence of demesne lordship on the economy of villagers, particularly tenant farming, and their standards of living. These chapters investigate whether it is justified to associate early modern East-Central and Eastern Europe with a general economic backwardness from a comparative European perspective. In this respect, the new perspective 'from the village' comes fully to bear in that it concentrates on the commercial nature of the tenant economic sphere and on standards of living of the rural population. It thus helps to overcome earlier pessimistic generalisations about the poor state of a market-averse peasant economy and society, intended to buttress the analytical divide between a 'progressive' (Western) and a 'backward' (Eastern) Europe.

2 The Myth of a Second Serfdom

[i] Introduction

The idea of a dualism in the agrarian development of Europe is strongly linked to the assumption that there existed a monolithic 'second serfdom' in Eastern Europe from circa 1500 up to the emancipation of the rural population in the late eighteenth and nineteenth centuries. Based on recent advances in empirical research, this chapter will systematically question and criticise previous characterisations of this alleged system and of the social and economic situation of the rural population within it. There emerges considerable regional variation in the practice of the seignorial system of demesne lordship, which is in contradiction to traditional descriptions of 'serfdom' and 'subjection'. The process of the establishment of demesne lordship occurred in stages and lasted over a long period, from the middle of the fifteenth until the second half of the seventeenth century (or until the eighteenth century in Russia). It was traditionally characterised by the assumption that villagers' personal and property rights were severely weakened. However, there was significant variation between the individual territories and over time in this respect. More recent research has identified important areas of autonomy and independent action among villagers and in their communities, which challenges the idea that the asymmetric relationship between villagers and lords resulted in the former's complete suppression in early modern East-Central and Eastern Europe.

[ii]   The Meaning of Serfdom and Subjection

In most of early modern Europe, farmers and smallholders were not the formal owners of the land they worked, but held it in tenure from a secular or church landlord. This system of land lordship originated in the medieval period and was based on rendering a rent in exchange for the use of the land. In the early modern period, the relationship in which lords still held dominion over their tenants was primarily constituted through the tenure of land. The resulting domination or subjection was thus primarily tenurial in nature, limited to the land tenure and not including the personal bondage of the tenant [34, 110, 116].

By contrast, the distinctive feature of serfdom was a personal bondage between the serf and his overlord in addition to their tenurial relationship. In this respect, an overlord often united powers of lordship over the land tenure (landlordship) with those of lordship over jurisdiction (jurisdictional lordship, aspects of banal lordship) and personal lordship [115]. As opposed to a purely tenurial relationship, serfs could be relocated without their tenures, for example from one estate to another. We can find such cases in areas in which full serfdom developed during the early modern period, such as parts of the Duchies of Schleswig-Holstein, Mecklenburg or Western Pomerania, even though they were sometimes officially banned, and in Russia [22, 45, 123, 126, 218]. They also occurred in Estonia and Livonia (Northern Latvia and Estonia) [99, 100], the Principalities of Moldavia and Wallachia, and apparently also in Hungary and Transylvania. However, in these countries serfdom did not become established [155, 157].

The ability of serfs to conclude legally binding contracts is regarded as more limited than for the free or subject population, but they certainly maintained a legal personality (as opposed to outright slavery) and were able to seek court protection or defend customary rights by legal means [2, 25, 26, 123, 126]. Serfs were considered to be in hereditary bondage to their lord. Some eighteenth-century legal scholars even declared serfs, along with their land, to be the lord's property. Although such statements could influence contemporary debate, historical research is interested in the actual practice of the system, which rarely corresponded to the clear-cut views and ideologies of some remote elites. Even if serfs accepted their status, as the inhabitants of the Holstein village of Bokhorst did around 1700, they defended what they regarded as their rights. In this particular case, they insisted on customary property rights over their farmland. Economic considerations dominated serfdom and serfs *and* lords had rights and mutual obligations. This included the seignorial duty to care for serfs in times of distress, such as famines, for instance by accepting delay in rent payment or offering grain seed [25, 112, 126, 136, 225]. The available studies show conflicting evidence in this respect.

Given these characteristics, it is necessary to distinguish clearly between serfdom – that is, personal bondage and a status of unfreedom – on the one hand and forms of tenurial relations on the other (see [2] on this important distinction). I shall call the seignorial domination resulting from the tenure 'subjection'. For lack of a better word in English, this choice seems best to convey the meaning of the original terms (German *Untertänigkeit*; Czech *poddanství*; Slovak *poddanský stav*; Polish *poddaństwo*; Hungarian *jobbágyság*). In this system, tenants were regarded as 'subject' to their lords (but not as serfs) [3, 4, 34, 116].

In the case of hereditary subjection (German *Erbuntertänigkeit, Gutsuntertänigkeit*; Hungarian *örökös jobbágyság*), the relationship automatically extended to tenants' offspring. In most territories of East-Central and Eastern Europe, subjection developed into hereditary subjection during the sixteenth and seventeenth centuries. Only in certain areas, described in more detail below, did it turn into an extreme form as serfdom. Serfdom also existed in particular areas of Western Europe, but the burdens resulting from this status were mostly much lighter than those prevailing in the eastern part of the continent.

The fact that subjection could be hereditary contributes to its occasional confusion with serfdom. In subjection, seignorial domination always remained tied to the tenure, even though demesne lords deliberately aimed at weakening the differences in practice, if this was to their own advantage. Hereditary subjects could buy themselves free from the tenurial relation, as could serfs from personal bondage. Demesne lords would confirm their release by means of a document (*Losbrief*), which would be handed over for a fee. For instance, Jürgen Kriese was called a 'free farmer' when he received a large tenure of four hides (a measure of landholding) of land in 1663; and Martin Trampe bought himself free from serfdom in his home estate in Pomerania for the considerable sum of 60 *reichstaler*, only voluntarily to accept the status of hereditary subjection when he bought a large farm in the Brandenburg Uckermark in 1667 [106]. Serfs and subjects would remain on an estate if it was sold to another lord. This illustrates that ultimately the relationship of subjection was less one of a personal nature to the lord, but rather one to his object of lordship, the estate; that is, to land and property.

All the other characteristics of serfdom quoted in the literature (restriction of mobility, compulsory employment of young adults in agricultural service on demesne farms, labour rents/*corvée* and lack of secure property rights [16]) could also accompany subjection within demesne lordship [44], especially if it was hereditary. This makes it even more important to differentiate carefully on the basis of the actual local conditions. Marxist approaches in particular favoured socio-economic factors over pure legal ones to define serfdom [16, 155]. For instance, extremely high levels of labour rents and the complete erosion of tenant property rights are regarded as indicators of extreme manifestations of demesne lordship or outright serfdom (see Section iv).

[iii]   Regional Realities

Around 1800, there was a large drive of rural reform launched by almost all the states and territories of Europe (Russia would follow last in 1861) finally to abolish ancien régime institutions and modernise agriculture to achieve the high returns observed, by experts and state administrators of the day, in regions of England, the Netherlands, the Lower Rhine, Schleswig-Holstein, Mecklenburg and others. The writings of enlightened reformers not only deliberately tended sometimes to confuse subjection and serfdom but also to victim- ise serfs and the economy of tenant farmers in order to justify the changes, and sometimes deliberately associated the status of such people with slavery to underline their message. Although this may have given some weight to their arguments, this association is also very wrong, and it therefore seems even more regrettable that it is sometimes repeated today in the scholarly literature. Many of the conventional images associated with subjection and serfdom, which also entered the scholarly historical literature, can be traced to these descriptions or to eighteenth-century conceptions of Eastern Europe [53]. Serfs were often stereotypically characterised with terms such as unhappy, lazy and stubborn; sometimes this was declared to be a result of the system whose powerless victims they were [26, 38, 54, 112, 120]. If we want to identify the burden and the economic consequences of serfdom, we have to cut through the layers of traditional characterisation that have built up in historical research and haunt some of today's surveys. These often present an undifferentiated picture of serfdom or fail to make the necessary distinctions in terms of their particular cases.

There were considerable discrepancies in how contemporaries understood the status of the rural population, even though in general lords were keen to use and extend their power to their own advantage [136]. In the 1740s, the Habsburg authorities considered introducing the emancipation of the rural population in the Czech Lands to secure their allegiance for the War of Austrian Succession (1740–48). In 1742, one of the highest-ranking government officials, himself the owner of vast estates in Bohemia, concluded that the status of the rural population as their lords' subjects derived from the fact that they did not own their land but were tenants of their landlords. As a consequence, they were obliged to render rents and forced labour. Thus, despite the fact that the equivalent to the term 'serfdom' was sometimes used in German-language documents, contemporary nobles claimed that villagers in Bohemia were not serfs and that there existed only a tenurial relationship, not personal bondage or unfreedom. Nevertheless, when Emperor Joseph II launched a major reform of the rural economy and society in territories of the Habsburg Monarchy, it included a law called the Serfdom Act for Bohemia and Moravia in 1781. This contradiction was apparent also to contemporaries, who used it against the act [75]. At the very same time, the Estates in Livonia were trying to convince the authorities of the Russian state, into which the country had been incorporated in the 1720s, that their rural tenants were indeed serfs without personal or property rights [97]. Despite the official designation of the rural population as serfs in mid-seventeenth-century Mecklenburg law codes, in the eighteenth century the Estates denied that their subjects were serfs. They probably had something to gain from presenting the condition of the rural population in a better light, if only to react against reformers who made serfdom and subjection responsible for economic problems [128]. Legal scholars, too, continuously reviewed the situation and their opinions often changed over time. Not least, in conflict situations the term 'serfdom' was used in a strategic manner. Villagers stated as a defence argument that any burden might be possible in a neighbouring territory, where the people were serfs [39], but that the treatment against which they were protesting was unheard of in their particular country. To complicate matters further, demesne lords, state authorities and sometimes even villagers would freely use the terms 'serf' and 'subject' (or 'hereditary subject') synonymously between the late sixteenth and the late eighteenth century, even in periods and territories in which serfdom had not been introduced by law. Depending on the context, they chose to interpret the rural population's status in the way they thought advantageous.

It can be difficult to draw a clear distinction between the harsher forms of (hereditary) subjection and serfdom. The border lines were sometimes indistinct with respect to everyday experiences. Despite this uncertainty, it does not seem analytically correct to me to group together the status of serfs and subjects, as is sometimes done even in recent surveys [4]. Contrary to the assumption of a general prevalence of serfdom, only in some areas did personal bondage or serfdom as defined above actually occur and be legally sanctioned by state or territorial law in the early modern period. Its establishment was usually a lengthy process. In certain territories, territorial laws and ordinances completed this development during the seventeenth century and gradually began to refer to the subject population as serfs. In most of East-Central and Eastern Europe, the process stopped short of serfdom and led to the establishment of different forms of subjection, as defined above.

The introduction of serfdom defined by law occurred in most of Mecklenburg (1645) as well as in Eastern (1616) and Western Pomerania (1645) [22, 132, 145]. In the Duchies of Schleswig-Holstein, nobles first pushed for serfdom in the sixteenth century, but the practice was only vaguely codified by law in 1614. In the diet, the prince agreed to acknowledge the existence of serfdom on noble estates and to send back fugitive serfs. In reality, this applied only to the (south-)eastern parts, representing about 25 per cent of the territory with a sixth of the population in 1803, where consolidated estates existed in which lords also held jurisdictional lordship. In practice, serfdom remained contested in Schleswig-Holstein, as the state tolerated the lords' claims rather than endorsed them and neither did the territory's constitution back the lords. Serfdom was not established in western and central parts of the country. In the west, landlord structures were in fact particularly weak and freehold farmers dominated [112, 126].

How far local conditions and the individual convictions of lords differed from each other can best be illustrated by the variation of opinions within one and the same powerful Holstein noble family. While one member regarded farmers 'always as his greatest enemies' and did not hesitate to kill three of them in 1722 and a second thought that literacy was not necessary for a serf in order to be a righteous subject, a third representative of the family abolished labour rents, granted hereditary tenure to his serfs in 1739 and distributed 5 per cent of his income among them every year, taking a patriarchal position as self-proclaimed 'father to all subjects'. An extreme view is also present in the statement of another lord in 1740, who responded to his serfs that 'nothing is yours, the soul belongs to God, your bodies, farms and everything you have is mine' [136].

The co-existence of serfdom and subjection in the same country also applies to Brandenburg, where conditions varied between milder forms of subjection, which dominated, and serfdom in particular areas. After 1640, demesne lords secured legal confirmation for their claim that the rural population were serfs in the districts of Uckermark (1643 and 1646), Neumark and the area of Crossen-Züllichau and Cottbus [104, 123]. Intensive research in the last 25 years has confirmed that, apart from a tendency to an increasing power of demesne lordship from west to east within the Electorate, there also existed important local variations. Within the same regions, there were estates and villages with tighter and looser forms of demesne lordship, with both a high proportion of demesne farming and its total absence [123].

The forced introduction of serfdom by law usually did not affect the entire population of a territory. In the eighteenth century, one third of the rural population of Western Pomerania were not serfs. At the same time, when conditions were tightened for villagers throughout Eastern Pomerania, demesne lords attracted farmers for new settlement activities in the east of the country. They received privileged status and secure property rights, and were partly free of subjection and bondage. After the Thirty Years' War, new tenants for the abandoned farmsteads were attracted with guarantees of their freedom in Mecklenburg. While in Mecklenburg-Strelitz most of the rural population were regarded as serfs by 1800, this did not apply to between a quarter and a third of the rural population in regions of the Duchy of Mecklenburg-Schwerin. In Brandenburg, extensive land-reclamation activities by the state guaranteed freedom and secure property rights for new settlers [110, 115, 123].

In the Duchy of (East) Prussia, sixteenth- and seventeenth-century documents speak of some groups of the rural population as serfs, yet the term came in disuse during the eighteenth century and was replaced by 'hereditary subject'. Not all rural inhabitants were automatically subjects, either. According to an analysis for three particular districts in 1784, 42 per cent of the tenant farmers were free. This proportion was usually even larger among that part of the rural population that did not perform labour rents. Then there was a privileged group who owned their farms in freehold and were all regarded as free. Towards the end of the eighteenth century, only about two-thirds of the total population in royal estates was in subject status [60, 170].

Although Russia has always been regarded as the classic example of rural serfdom (*крепостничество/krepostnichestvo*), a recent analysis raises doubts and shows that there was no definition of serfdom by state law between the seventeenth and the nineteenth centuries. In addition, the term as such does not appear in contemporary documents [226, 227]. There is no uniform assessment in existing surveys [208, 209, 210, 213, 214, 216, 218, 221, 224, 225]. The disagreement lies in the interpretation of the causes and consequences of the famous 1649 Law Code (*ulozhenie*), which was traditionally regarded as a decisive watershed for tightening seignorial relations. Whatever the position, one has to remember that these measures were extended by various other government decrees during the eighteenth and early nineteenth centuries (including also the newly acquired territories), while the demesne economy, which was the most important influence, grew systematically only after 1750. The strongest effects for villagers were thus to be expected only in the latter half of the period 1649–1861.

Even if we adopted the traditional reading, a brief quantitative survey would question the overall importance of serfdom. The total proportion of those members of the rural male population of European Russia usually classified as serfs declined from 53.9 per cent in 1695 to 39.2 per cent in 1858 [27, 209, 217, 225, 226].

By 1861, less than half of the villagers lived in noble estates (the rest were state tenants) and of this group, 55 per cent (or less than a quarter of all rural households) were exposed to demands for labour rents (*барщина, barshchina*), which for some could also be very limited [225]. The proportion varied regionally, so that serfs could represent the majority among rural households in some areas such as in the left-bank Ukraine. The other groups of the rural population, mainly state tenants, had different rights and duties; they were also bound to the soil, but they were not serfs [208, 216].

Villagers on private estates became fully regarded as serfs only just before the 1861 reforms. By this time, about half of them had succeeded in acquiring a different legal status by means of military service, being granted or purchasing their freedom, moving from their estate (officially or unofficially) or by other means [226]. This is not to question the drastic consequences of demesne lordship in areas of the Russian countryside, as evident in case studies particularly for noble estates [214, 223]. However, these conditions did not apply to the majority of the rural population, which makes it necessary to rethink the view of a general Russian rural serfdom.

The situation in Russia was also relevant for the Baltic territories that came under its rule. Although most of the literature classifies the rural population of seventeenth- and eighteenth-century Livonia and Estonia as serfs and links this development to the confirmation of seignorial privileges in 1561 and the regulations of 1668, 1676 and 1739 [34, 94, 97, 100, 170], this interpretation should be re-examined in future research, as personal serfdom was not introduced by state law. Attempts to limit demesne lords' powers over villagers were not confined to the Swedish period, but also occurred under Polish rule in the late sixteenth century. Moreover, it seems that the far-reaching 1561 privileges never passed through the Polish diet [95, 97, 99]. A declaration of the Swedish Governor General in 1671 may have been a decisive turning point [99, 100]. Legal texts of the 1720s and 1730s authored by the Livonian Estates did use the term 'serfs' for the rural population, but were merely interpretations of the relevant seventeenth-century Swedish laws and, moreover, show striking differences in their views on the actual rights of demesne lords over their villagers. Moreover, these legal statements were never signed into binding law by the Russian authorities. Depending on the region, between 6 and 25 per cent of rural households were situated on state estates in the late eighteenth and early nineteenth centuries, which, as in Russia, could make a significant difference to their status and seignorial burdens [14]. For the Polish Commonwealth, too, views about the personal bondage of the rural population seem incorrect. Andrzej Wyczański emphasises that villagers and their communities maintained the rights and the ability to take part in legal transactions, which does not correspond to a status of personal serfdom [115, 201]. For a characterisation of the agrarian structure, Polish historiography does not usually use the terms 'serfdom' or 'serf', but refers to demesne lordship as *ustrój/gospodarka folwarczno-pańszczyzniany* (demesne lordship/economy based on labour rents) and to the status of the villagers as *poddaństwo* (subjection). Attracting settlers in the sixteenth and seventeenth centuries led to a growing group of privileged or free villagers (by 1791 nearly 16 per cent of the total rural population and 25 per cent of the rural population in Great Poland). For instance, in the area of Royal Prussia, the establishment of demesnes remained limited and tenant farmers and village communities retained a high degree of independence [115, 161, 170]. It is therefore unlikely that a uniform system was established in the Polish Commonwealth, given the pronounced internal structural differences (for instance, a strong dominance of large magnate landholdings existed in the Grand Duchy of Lithuania as opposed to the dominance of the petty gentry, many even without subject tenants, in some parts of Poland) and the uneven development of the demesne economy, which was very limited in parts of Royal Prussia, Little Poland, Lithuania and the Ukraine [95, 170, 221].

From the 1530s onwards, the Kingdom of Hungary (including Croatia, Transylvania and present-day Slovakia) was divided under Ottoman and Habsburg rule as well as an autonomous part in the Transylvanian area. In general, the rural population was not subjected to serfdom in the Ottoman Empire and in the Habsburg part of it subjection and not serfdom developed. According to Hungarian historiography, villagers in demesne lordship (*nagybirtok*, literally latifundium) were in (hereditary) subjection. Among the dominant approaches before 1989 (see Chapter 1, Section ii), some historians interpreted the situation as serfdom, but others strongly disagreed even then. Thus, in Hungarian research as well, the idea of a 'second serfdom' was not generally accepted. The establishment of the demesne economy remained incomplete until the eighteenth century. A substantial proportion of the rural population – in certain areas even all of it – were free to move. The inhabitants of numerous privileged agricultural market towns, which were a specific characteristic of Hungarian rural society, formed a separate group with certain liberties. In individual counties, a rather large proportion of the rural population lived in such settlements. Until 1750, landlord structures were particularly weak on the huge Hungarian plains, an area slowly resettled after the retreat of the Ottoman Empire, where tenants could get access to land with personal liberties under secure terms [14, 51, 151, 153, 155, 158, 159].

Traditional claims about serfdom in Ottoman territories of South-Eastern Europe seem to be without foundation. In the Principalities of Moldavia and Wallachia, rural relations were regarded as the strictest within the Ottoman Empire, but recent studies show convincingly that serfdom did not develop. While mobility restrictions were imposed, all other characteristics of hereditary subjection (such as jurisdictional rights of lords or considerable labour rents) were not systematically established. There were frequent state interventions in landlord relations in favour of villagers. Demesne farming did not develop widely before the late eighteenth century [150, 157].

In Denmark, lords acquired the right to use tenant labour rents from the late Middle Ages. In 1523–36 they received the privilege of legal jurisdiction over their villagers. With the expansion of demesne farming on noble estates after 1550, labour rents increased until the eighteenth century. Forms of subjection that included movement restrictions (*vornedskabet*) occurred only in Zealand from about the 1490s onwards and were lifted in 1702. The introduction of new restrictions for the male population in 1733 (*stavnsbåndet*) was not linked to lordship but was a measure by the state for military reasons. In most church and royal estates, but also in many noble ones, lordship was mainly based on cash rents, so that ultimately there was no predominance of demesne lordship [14, 88, 139]. A significant share of bourgeois landed property was a distinctive feature of conditions in Denmark [14, 88].

Subjection spread into the southern Swedish province of Scania, which belonged to Denmark until 1658. Despite seignorial pressure, however, formal mobility restrictions were not established.

A mixed seignorial system prevailed, because only slightly more than half of the tenant farms were located in estates with demesne structures in the eighteenth century [90, 91]. In the other parts of Sweden, the establishment of demesne farming remained the exception and in certain regions very little land and few estates were noble property. Tenant farmers on noble land were subject to seignorial jurisdiction, lacked secure property rights, paid feudal dues and possibly rendered labour rents, whereas tenants on crown land paid rent to the king and freeholders were free owner-occupiers who were only obliged to pay state taxes. In Finland, a demesne economy was not established on a systematic basis and at the height of the Swedish nobility's power, fewer villagers were under noble control in Finland than in Sweden proper (58 per cent vs 65 per cent in 1650). A state policy of maintaining the rural tax base meant that stricter forms of subjection remained limited to the province of Scania and the Swedish territories at the southern coastline of the Baltic Sea.

In the historical Czech Lands (comprising Bohemia, Moravia, Upper Lusatia and Silesia), serfdom and personal bondage did not develop and were not codified in territorial law. With the exception of Upper Silesia and certain areas of Upper Lusatia [103], the form of demesne lordship arising during the sixteenth century is usually counted among the milder variants from a comparative perspective. The literature concludes that for several parts of Bohemia, Moravia and Lower Silesia the demesne economy did not develop as strongly as in other East-Elbian territories. Like in most other territories of the area, formal mobility restrictions were established for the subject population and labour rents existed, although, exceptions aside, they usually did not reach levels usual in areas of stricter forms of subjection. Most importantly, the hereditary property rights of the rural population were widely maintained, although forms of leasehold spread in a minority of areas in Bohemia and Upper Lusatia after the Thirty Years' War. Although Czech research before 1989 used the term 'second serfdom' (*druhé nevolnictví*), historians always stressed that its development in Bohemia, Moravia and Silesia had special characteristics and resembled the western system of seignorialism until 1620–50. The terms *velkostatek* (literally latifundium) and subjection (*poddanství*) were often preferred to describe the situation [1, 20, 80, 85]. In most recent Czech research, the use of the concept of serfdom has been largely abandoned.

The survey of research in this section thus questions the idea that a (second) serfdom existed all over East-Elbian Europe. Leaving Russia aside, we can find areas in which serfdom was established in Schleswig-Holstein, Mecklenburg, Pomerania and possibly in Livonia and Estonia, but in Brandenburg serfdom existed in certain districts only [34] and it was not a necessary part of demesne lordship in East-Elbian territories. In his seminal study, Georg Friedrich Knapp differentiates between territories with 'genuine' (lack of legal personality) as well as 'not genuine' serfdom (villagers with insecure property rights but without personal bondage) and those with subjection, where mobility restrictions applied but secure property rights prevailed [22, 25, 26, 106]. The actual level of labour rents (*corvée*) was sometimes used to distinguish between regions of subjection and its extreme manifestations, which could also lead to serfdom. Quite similar to the list just presented, the regions with extreme labour rent obligations beyond three days a week per full tenant farmholding included regions of the Duchies of Schleswig-Holstein, Mecklenburg and Western (Swedish) Pomerania. To this classification by Gerhard Heitz, Hartmut Harnisch added Estonia and Latvia (Livonia) as well as parts of the Electorate of Brandenburg [17].

The practice of serfdom thus varied greatly over time. Even where it was legally sanctioned, it was not established by a single act and, once established, would not last unchanged until peasant emancipation. On the contrary, it developed gradually, was only installed for a very limited period and its practical consequences were continually shifting. Under no circumstances and for no territory, therefore, we can speak of the whole early modern period as an age of a second serfdom, let alone Eastern Europe as a whole.

[iv]   Subjection in Demesne Lordship

Mobility restrictions

Mobility restrictions were one of the earliest ways of weakening villagers' rights [16, 22, 36, 48, 207]. In this respect, one wave of legal action can be observed as a consequence of the crisis of the late Middle Ages, when lords and princes struggled to maintain a population of rent-paying tenants. They tried to define the conditions governing migration in order to prevent those owing dues to their lords from moving. The basic right of movement after the fulfilment of all obligations was not questioned and was in fact confirmed, such as in Prussia in 1445 and 1482, in Brandenburg in 1383 and 1518 and in Hungary until 1514. This is also assumed for Poland [106, 158, 207]. For instance, Prussian regulations in 1417–20 restricted movement prior to settlement of debts with the lord and finding another tenant to replace one's position. When these laws were re-issued (1445, 1466–7, 1478, 1482) they still explicitly confirmed that tenants were free to move under certain conditions. Finally, full restrictions were passed in the East Prussian Land Ordinance of 1526 [36, 47].

That diets repeated such regulations is sometimes quoted as evidence that mobility restrictions could not be enforced (see Table 2.1). For instance, economically powerful and politically independent cities could resist the extradition of rural runaways. Studies on

Table 2.1 Chronology of the establishment of mobility restrictions

Country	Year
Moravia	1390, 1486, 1575
(East) Prussia	1417, 1526, 1577
Poland	1420, 1496, 1500, 1501, 1526
Bohemia	1437, 1479, 1487, 1500, 1575
Schleswig	1461, 1614
Denmark (Zealand)	c.1490
Russia	1497, 1649
Livonia	1508
Hungary	1514, 1608
Mecklenburg	1516, 1572
Holstein	1524
Lithuania	1529, 1554, 1566, 1588
Brandenburg	1536
Upper Lusatia	1551
Wallachia	1595
Pomerania	1616
Moldavia	1620s, 1646

Note: Dates give the first mention and/or the implementation of mobility restrictions.
Source: [5].

23

the sixteenth century find considerable migration – also seasonal – among the rural population [82, 201]. The literature sometimes concludes that fifteenth- or early sixteenth-century territorial princes or demesne lords lacked the means to police such restrictions.

This fails to do justice to the fact that legal restrictions were almost universal in the area and were part of a long-term development that in the end could drastically reduce the mobility and legal status of villagers when occurring together with other characteristics of demesne lordship. As already indicated, the original regulations were not intended to ban movement of tenants per se. However, later restrictions, with a different purpose, were able to build on these. Recurring regulation does not primarily relate to limited possibilities of control, but rather reflected the fact that aims may have shifted over time and that corresponding changes were applied to the re-issued regulations. The composite nature of some of the states meant that legislation was not institutionalised everywhere at the same time and that interests among the Estates in the different parts of the area diverged. Thus, the Hungarian restrictions of 1514 did not apply in the same manner to Wallachia (where Estates confirmed the basic right of movement but introduced a levy of a large quantity of grain) or Transylvania.

Measures at first targeted tenant farmers, so a considerable minority of the rural population was not affected and was able to migrate, for example for wage work. We should thus not be surprised to find a highly mobile section of the rural population, particularly certain social and occupational groups, until at least 1600 or even throughout the early modern period [14, 95, 207], which is part of the movement that studies denying the immediate effects of restriction noticed. In addition, these codes did not ban movement as such, but linked it to seeking seignorial consent in exchange for a fee. They addressed a problem of enforcement among the members of the Estates and diets themselves: when receiving tenants who had escaped from elsewhere, lords had the incentive for opportunistic behaviour and for undermining existing regulations by not sending them back. The introduction of fines for permission to leave is linked to this problem as well, because, theoretically, these could have been paid either by the villagers prior to leaving or by their new lords.

The right of villagers to leave after paying all obligations was common in the later Middle Ages, but, depending on custom, lords could insist on their finding a replacement. The first restrictive measures must therefore be understood as reminders to stick to these rules, when depopulation and crisis made it more difficult to find adequate individuals for those who had left, fled from war or migrated to the towns, and not as undermining the right to move per se. The first restrictions on movement in Russia in the 1450s specifically applied to tenants of monasteries only (extended to all villages in 1497), who were indebted and were thus allowed to move only on St George's Day (26 November) [213]. The first fifteenth-century regulations in Poland were also primarily specifications regarding the conditions for *leaving* an estate. This situation continued as a pattern for later regulations and as a legitimisation for increasing restrictions. When in the period around 1500 Mecklenburg demesne lords really tried to prevent tenants to leave, they argued that the tenants had not paid their rents properly, were indebted to the lords and hence were not allowed to move away [129].

To justify their demands, the Estates occasionally claimed that villagers consistently violated the conditions under which they were free to migrate and that therefore lords and (on request from diets and Estates) the prince had to intervene. This can be seen most clearly in fifteenth-century Livonia, where lords complained that tenants failed to fulfil their obligations before leaving. Restrictive measures were meant to force cities or lords either to send back fugitives or to pay their debts for them. Transfer payments among lords are indeed recorded. It appears that the explicit restriction of mobility only emerged in the 1510s, although in fact this shift in legislation was aimed at addressing a different problem. As it turned out, settlement procedures between lords caused many lengthy and expensive negotiations until the debts of former tenants were finally settled. Therefore the law turned from the original principle of 'either man or debt' to a new, less expensive one, which was the strict obligation to send fugitives back [14, 95, 100]. The fact that mobility restrictions in Livonia did not apply to villagers of crown estates until at least the early seventeenth century [95] also illustrates that the lack of cooperation among noble lords was a main contributor to the problem.

A second wave of such regulations occurred in land ordinances in the upheaval after the seventeenth-century wars. Thousands of applications for movement and strict measures by individual demesne lords suggest that the bans were widely imposed, but also faced problems. Practices varied considerably. For some lords, the procedures for granting a certificate of release (*Losbrief*) were a formality for which they could collect another fee. Conditions after the mid-seventeenth century prohibited strict application of the law. Because of population decline, noble and princely estates, for instance in Estonia, Livonia and Courland, were unwilling to send back fugitives, whose total number was estimated at around 5 per cent of the population in the 1710s. After 1650, Swedish authorities did not rein in the migration of villagers, which may also have contributed to higher rates of movement. Obeying the legislation to return fugitives happened more systematically only after the situation consolidated during the 1750s [95, 100].

Low population density and loose landlord control could prevent stricter policing of the law, such as in parts of Hungary. In Poland or Russia, flight and starting a new existence in areas of settlement expansion (which was often helped by certain privileges, such as years free of rents and tax) could not be effectively controlled. Apart from the impact of political conflicts and wars, flight probably was a widespread means of resistance against demesne lordship or tax burdens, but hope of a better life at the destination was also a pull. Holstein fugitives longed for the less seignorialised western parts of the country, moved on to Holland or were attracted by the chances offered by the major port cities of Hamburg and Lübeck [100, 170, 221, 225]. The overall estimate that about 5 per cent of the total taxable population were fugitives in Russia between 1727 and 1741 (526 000 were found and returned between 1719 and 1742) cannot be interpreted as the result of the pressures of demesne lordship alone. As in other territories, it would be wrong to assume that migration was only illegal. On the contrary, data for 11 Russian provinces show that a total of 105 500 villagers migrated by order or with the consent of their lords, while nearly 65 000 were fugitives [216].

While some lords were relaxed, many were concerned about these developments. For instance, for certain types of movement such as for marriage, lords frequently granted permission freely and in a reciprocal way. In contrast, seignorial complaints in Upper Lusatia increased dramatically within a few years after 1650 and one estimate referred to about 2000 fugitives [103]. Fugitives represented a strong concern of Schleswig-Holstein demesne lords and were also persecuted. Estonian lords systematically began to search for the villagers who had left their estates during the wars and sued each other to return fugitives [100]. The administration of the royal estates in Bohemia (estates of the Bohemian chamber) interfered little with short-term or seasonal migration of individuals, but long-term migration, such as for taking up an apprenticeship or permanent leave, was subject to permission and the chamber repeatedly warned the local administration to maintain strict controls. There is mixed evidence on the effects of this, however. On the one hand, the administration recorded only a few villagers leaving for good without permission. As permission was granted for a fee, the financial incentive also played a role in surveillance. On the other hand, there were phases in which permission was only given in a restrictive manner. In periods of vacant tenancies, for instance, no grants were issued to residing tenants. Fees could be used as instruments in this respect and were then sometimes quite arbitrary and high [80]. Demesne lords elsewhere also used fees as a restriction, such as in late sixteenth-century Brandenburg, when there was an increase in the fee necessary to gain permission to leave. When the lords needed money, they were ready to release their subjects even in times of demographic crisis. But even as late as the end of the eighteenth century, microhistorical evidence reveals that it could still take more effort to be allowed to move away in Brandenburg than merely paying a sum of money [106, 124].

It seems that the local context was decisive for the imposition of mobility restrictions. Even in the seventeenth and eighteenth centuries, when state and seignorial authorities were strongest, mobility restrictions did not prevent the regular seasonal movement of thousands of labourers. Studies on property transfers also demonstrate considerable local or regional movement [73, 85]. Mobility of the rural population throughout early modern Europe has long been underestimated in historiography and the conclusion that migration and movement were ordinary patterns and occurred very widely indeed has only recently emerged. There is no reason to believe that Eastern Europe was different. Individual life courses show frequent movement and a succession of livelihoods in different places. Finally, one has to consider the vast dimensions of the estate properties of princes or the higher nobility. Movement from one estate to another belonging to the same lord must be regarded as normal.

27

Courts and the legal system

The question of access to and control of courts or jurisdictional institutions relates to the legal dimension of (hereditary) subjection [22]. Although village communities maintained control over the so-called lower jurisdictional sphere (such as neighbourhood conflicts, real estate transactions or minor offences), demesne lords frequently controlled higher jurisdictions (major offences).

One of the reasons for this shift of powers originally held by princes may have been chronic fiscal difficulties, which forced rulers to transfer powers and sell or pawn princely property to the Estates, or to grant the Estates' wishes in exchange for their consent to taxation plans [22, 129]. As characteristic as the coincidence of lordship over land and over the jurisdictional sphere was for demesne lordship [123], it was neither universal nor with homogeneous consequences for the rural population. For instance, in Schleswig-Holstein all noble lords received the privilege of legal jurisdiction in 1524, but in practice this was only executed in the areas where consolidated estate property had evolved during the later Middle Ages [136, 139].

The consequences of demesne lordship could be particularly strong in the territories in which villagers were denied access to royal or princely courts in legal conflicts with their lords. In this respect, the Estates sometimes lobbied successfully to restrict villagers' access to the highest princely jurisdiction. In 1518, villagers outside crown estates in Poland lost the privilege of appeal to royal courts, although in certain matters they could still appeal to regional state courts [115, 170, 201]. While villagers were denied the right to state court action against their lords in Bohemia in the later Middle Ages, they retained the right to file protests in the form of petitions, which were then investigated. In 1680 responsibility for these petitions was given to the state district administrators and formal procedures were established in 1704 [80]. In Brandenburg, where demesne lords wanted to restrict their villagers' right to appeal in 1527, the rural population and the margrave's Court of the Chamber simply would not enforce this [123]. Extended legal battles between villagers and lords became a special characteristic of Brandenburg demesne lordship and by no means did the court always rule in favour of the lords' interests [106].

Property rights

Among the most important legal and economic characteristics that separate the status of subjection from that of serfdom are property rights. Subjection could be accompanied by secure hereditary property rights (such as hereditary tenure or hereditary leasehold, comparable also to copyhold) but also by less secure forms of tenure, such as leasehold for life or for a certain number of years [16]. Legally, hereditary tenure, although often including full rights of disposal, was a usufruct, which is the right to use the land permanently (*dominium utile*), as opposed to full ownership in the modern sense. Ultimately, the ownership (*dominium directum*) and the use rights were the privilege of landlords, who devolved the use rights to their tenants in exchange for rent obligations. The complete denial of any form of *de iure* property rights is a characteristic element of serfdom to which early modern documents frequently refer, although serfs often did have informal or customary rights.

Recent advances in research suggest that contrary to previous accounts, secure property rights among the rural population were the rule rather than the exception in demesne lordship. What is uncontested is that hereditary property rights of tenant farms and smallholdings were practically universal in the late medieval period. The later existence of insecure property rights, caused by developments beginning in the sixteenth century, cannot be denied, but they were often confined regionally or to a specific period. Associated with this, the extent of the expropriation of tenant farms (*Bauernlegen*) to increase demesne farmland has traditionally been overstated (see Chapter 4, Section ii). Secure property rights (forms of hereditary tenure) dominated in early modern Bohemia, Moravia and Lower Silesia (and also in many regions of Upper Lusatia) [85], Poland/Lithuania [95, 161, 167], many regions of the Electorate of Brandenburg [109, 123] and in Schleswig-Holstein outside the core zones of the demesne economy [36]. In Hungary, tenants' hereditary use rights were largely maintained (if not legally then in practice), although sales and alienation may have been restricted. There existed secure and largely unrestricted special property rights over vineyards [151, 153]. Practices in Denmark and Sweden offered security for tenants [14] and tenants held hereditary rights over their farmsteads in Livonia until at least 1600. During the seventeenth century the transfer of tenures to heirs also seems to have been usual [95, 100]. In several territories there existed larger groups of freehold farmers (owner-occupiers).

In many regions of Russia, structures of tenurial relations were entirely different. In the early modern period a system of communal land repartition spread, in which land was periodically re-assigned among households. Russian farmers received continuous access to land according to the productive and financial capabilities of their households (for the repartitional commune in Russia see [209, 210, 224, 225]). Villagers' subsistence was based on a form of entitlement to land and consequently tenurial conflicts with lords hardly ever arose [210, 214]. Restrictions on disposal rights over the land of tenants are occasionally recorded, such as in the western Ukraine in the eighteenth century.

In a number of countries from the sixteenth century onwards, tenants' property rights eroded to a certain extent due to landlord pressure. In a long process, tenants' rights of free disposal in Mecklenburg were reduced. A settlement in 1621 declared all villagers' landholding to be leases at will of the lord, unless tenants could present written documents that their tenures were hereditary [128, 132]. Yet in the district of Ratzeburg, hereditary tenure continued to exist throughout the seventeenth and eighteenth centuries; a better tenurial position is also assumed for the estate of the monastery of Dobbertin [22, 128]. In the Duchies of Western and Eastern Pomerania, hereditary tenure was abolished by the 'Peasants' and shepherds' ordinance', published in Eastern Pomerania in 1616 and introduced in Western Pomerania in 1645 [145]. Tenures were downgraded to leasehold at will of the lord. In practice, this did not exclude tenant families transmitting their holdings between generations. Transmission by way of inheritance or sale was also usual in Schleswig-Holstein demesne estates, even though tenants lacked formal property rights [125].

In Brandenburg, the occurrence and spread of leasehold at will (*Laßbesitz*) in the sixteenth century was a significant development. On the one hand, it can be interpreted in the context of a more general attempt to undermine villagers' property rights; on the other, however, it was only a practical means introduced specifically for new tenures on deserted land, for which lords had to provide initial investments, because tenants were unable or unwilling to do so. Nevertheless, hereditary tenure continued to dominate, for instance in two-thirds of the villages of the district of Prignitz in the beginning of the seventeenth century [109]. In the districts of Uckermark and Beeskow/Storckow, short-term leases for three or six years were established, for which tenants usually paid high rents. Often the tenures were held continuously, because lords were interested in stability among tenants. By contrast, princely estates partly attracted new tenants by guaranteeing hereditary tenure for their efforts to rebuild farms and villages after 1650. Individual noble lords followed a similar path when they offered to new tenants the possibility of remaining free and not burdened with any labour rents. In desperate attempts to raise cash, the lords granted hereditary tenure to leaseholders against certain payments. Indeed, the possibilities seemed unlimited for successful tenants, because in several cases they actually acquired properties in freehold. Other tenants guessed (correctly) that there was little danger of them being expropriated despite formally precarious leasehold rights and they turned down offers to buy hereditary tenure for their holdings [122]. According to a survey taken in princely estates in the Electorate in 1747/48, 46.9 per cent of 10 680 tenant farmers and smallholders held hereditary property rights [106, 109, 115, 123].

The trend after the Thirty Years' War towards weakening property rights in favour of limited leaseholds in Brandenburg, parts of Upper Lusatia or Bohemia (or after the Northern War in Estonia and Livonia) [17, 22, 85, 100, 103] must be interpreted in the context of this period. Population decreases, lack of capital among tenants and the need for a recovery of the economy forced lords to invest in farms and attract new tenants. Correspondingly, tenants did not have to purchase these holdings, because land, buildings and inventory remained seignorial property. Many even preferred short-term leases, because it guaranteed them freedom of mobility as the lord could not force them to find a replacement or to carry on after the contract ended [94, 108].

There is compelling evidence to conclude that secure property rights for tenants were preserved in the majority of regions of early modern East-Elbian demesne lordship. Where tenures were weakened in favour of leaseholds, practices or court rules often prevented severe negative consequences. Even in areas of serfdom, where formal property rights possibly did not apply, villagers could fall back on customary claims to their tenures [112].

Labour rents (*corvée*)

Labour rents were widespread throughout medieval Europe but, with the possible exception of regions of England, were usually very limited in the later Middle Ages. In East-Central and Eastern Europe, the rule was that a small number of days per year for each farm holding were allocated to ploughing and carting or manual work on demesne fields. According to many researchers, labour rents represented the key economic element of early modern demesne lordship. It was the demands of the expanding commercial demesne economy based on the systematic exploitation of tenant labour that caused the most important conflicts over resources [16, 17, 119]. Accordingly, research differentiated on the basis of the actual burden of labour rents between 'mild' forms of demesne lordship and 'harsh' ones (the border line being obligations of less or more than three days a week per tenant farm, up to unlimited ones, or *ungemessen*; see Chapter 4, Section iv). Although there are good reasons for such an approach, there is a danger that a comparison between territories ignores regional variations, which also occurred in areas within 'harsh' demesne lordship and serfdom.

Sixteenth- and seventeenth-century ordinances established that demesne lords could hire the teenage children of their tenants for service on their demesne farms (*Gesindezwang*; the regulations were often called servants' ordinances). Service was usually limited to three or at maximum five years and servants received wages for their work. Nevertheless, this form of exploitation is an important symbol of subjection due to demesne lordship (although it also occurred in territories west of the river Elbe).

The demesne economy

A further characterization of demesne lordship is based on the demesne economy and its role in seignorial income [111]. In the West of Europe, landlord income was usually based on cash rents, property transfer fees and fines. By 1600, such payments were often insignificant for demesne lords in East-Central and Eastern Europe. Instead, they frequently derived between two-thirds and nine-tenths of their annual income from operating a commercial demesne economy, consisting of demesne arable farming (often the major activity), animal husbandry (sheep and cattle), pisciculture and 'industrial' activities directly related to this agricultural basis, such as beer brewing or distilling (see Chapter 4, Sections iii, v and vi). In some regions in the Czech Lands, Silesia, Poland or Russia, demesne lords also invested in proto-industrial enterprises such as textile manufacture or iron production, especially in the eighteenth and early nineteenth centuries.

However, a full development of the demesene economy was not a universal pattern. Parts of Lower Silesia, Upper Lusatia or certain regions in Poland, Bohemia and Moravia, as well as large areas of central and northern Russia, are conventionally identified as areas in which many estates had only limited demesne activities. In addition, demesnes were far from being a phenomenon limited to East Elbian areas [14, 21, 111].

[v]   The View from Below

Serfdom and subjection represented asymmetric power relation-ships that were often accompanied by harsh realities for villagers. Yet earlier approaches to research made the mistake of thinking that villagers were mere victims, overwhelmed by the limitless domination of their lords. In fact the development of demesne lordship was hardly linear and continuous. If the local balance of power tipped towards lords or they ignored laws and court rules, cases of abuse can be encountered in the literature. It is necessary, however, to interpret these as particular cases within a wide spectrum of concrete manifestations of the seignorial system in early modern East Elbia. And these cases, as has been emphasised already, were also determined by villagers [6, 38, 108]. Seignorial powers were thus hardly limitless, but checked by village as well as state institutions. Based on this understanding of demesne lordship as a 'social model' [40], we arrive at a characterisation of subjec-tion and serfdom and its consequences that is very different from traditional approaches.

The following examples illustrate that systems of subjection or serfdom would not have worked without a minimum of cooperation and acceptance by villagers and their institutions. In many instances this set a limit to what demesne lords could do. Most importantly, demesne lordship stands for economic exploitation of the rural population. Traditional views stressed constant interference in the economy of tenant farmers and smallholders. Yet, obvious negative effects aside, villagers' market links were strong and they were able to produce a considerable surplus. The lords did not systematically interfere in the everyday management of tenant farms and households. Due to the possible existence of seignorial monopolies, they could sometimes supervise marketing to the benefit of their own privileged market towns or trading activities. Recent research points out that villagers had several means of avoiding regulations and that the real effects of interference could be negligible. Overall, villagers maintained a high degree of independence of household decision making in economic affairs (see Chapter 5, Section ii) [72, 84, 85, 108, 119].

Property rights and the transfer of property among villagers represent further areas in which the influence of demesne lords has usually been described as strong. The survey in Section iv demonstrated that the maintenance of tenants' property rights seemed to have been the rule in most territories. Systematic empirical inquiries into the transfer of tenant properties among villagers started in the 1960s and are among the strongest evidence we have for villagers' independent decision making. There certainly were reasons for seignorial interest and supervision in this respect, because the economic success of tenures guaranteed a constant flow of rents and labour to lords and demesnes. Seignorial administrators sometimes messed with villagers' strategies, but at least part of the interference in tenant property transfers can be explained, because villagers themselves called for seignorial intervention in conflicts with contract partners [85]. Despite the frequent existence of formal regulations, actual interference or overruling sales agreed among villagers remained the exception. Independent transfers of limited leaseholds can also be observed frequently, so the handling of formally different types of tenure was similar in practice. Even in areas of serfdom without formal tenant property rights, transfers of tenures remained largely within the autonomous sphere of villagers [7, 69, 72, 73, 85, 87, 167, 178, 186, 210].

Having identified areas in which villagers maintained independence to a large degree, rural power relations were nevertheless characterised by everyday conflict and insubordination. Village communities, aldermen, jurors and headmen could have an important role in this respect. As representatives, they demonstrated the collective nature of protest. There is no doubt that lords tried to weaken village communities and their institutions, control communal life (by state ordinances or seignorial instructions) and draw on communal resources. Yet, quite in contradiction to the usual argument that the lords succeeded [1], communes maintained autonomy and a decisive role in some respects of local administration (judicial, policing) and particularly in protests and conflicts [85, 107, 112, 116, 210, 214, 219].

Conflicts could arise for many reasons [41, 44, 112, 135, 214]. As labour rents were the most burdening and despised features of subjection and serfdom, resistance and open revolt frequently concentrated on these. Insubordination was widespread and included appearing late, sending lame and incapable workers or draught animals, working slowly, shirking or refusing to render services, and was often connected with long and difficult legal battles against lords to show and prove that an attempted increase of labour rents was against long-established custom [38, 39]. Supervisors in Holstein complained in 1740 that farmers sent girls for harvest work although they had deliberately ordered adult male servants or the farmers themselves. Everyday resistance could also be directed against all other form of exactions, quite frequently including state taxes [106, 112, 116, 123, 124, 125, 135, 170, 214].

Accordingly, lords, chief estate managers/stewards and also many contemporary printed manuals complained about the slack performance of labour rents. If demesne lords wanted to prevent this, they had to hire supervisors. On one day in 1629, the amazing number of nine officials were on a control mission in a Brandenburg field when they noticed that a young woman and her brother were working badly. Immediately, the young woman received a lashing, causing her brother to wave his scythe and to threaten 'to kill the supervisor' who had beaten her [43, 116]. Lords had ways to avoid or limit supervision costs. Russian estate owners, for instance, were often helped by family patriarchs and bailiffs or the village oligarchy to enforce social control in exchange for maintaining their influence. This cooperation based on shared interests also helped to stabilise subjection and the social system [81, 135, 210, 214, 220]. Lords needed villagers' cooperation to enforce the system, which means that villagers and their institutions had an important part in shaping it [40, 85, 116, 135, 215].

Conflicts between villagers and estate officials did not only occur frequently, but were at least occasionally strong and marked by violence. Russian estate managers and supervisors controlled villagers and responded to insubordination with floggings and other punishment [210, 214]. When servants complained against a supervisor on a Holstein estate in 1730, he replied that their protests would hardly matter even if he 'beat one of them to cripple' [136]. Given this situation, villagers themselves used violence or tried to bribe officials in order to avoid labour rents or burdens demanded by the state [135, 210, 214].

Labour rents were only one area of everyday conflict between lords and villagers. Others leading to open or concealed arguments involved competition about resources (lakes, fishing waters, pastures) [38], forced agricultural service of teenagers, mobility restrictions or security of tenure. In all these respects, village, seignorial and state courts could be important means of conflict resolution [85, 107]. Not only subjects but also serfs remained legal personalities and had the right to appear before a court or to conclude formal contracts; they also had personal property and an independent livelihood by means of their holdings or craft. For them, court protection could be particularly relevant to preserve custom. The literature agrees that villagers engaged in long, tedious and very expensive court battles against their lords [112, 116, 124, 125], who were hardly amused. Lords, too, could carry legal battles to the extreme and in individual cases, in which they took on other lords, parts of their families, parishes, town and village communities at the same time, the pursuit could ruin them financially [135]. The courts did intervene in cases of violence. When Uckermark demesne lords geared up their pressure against villagers after 1650, once it had been established that they were serfs, courts repeatedly intervened to protect individuals. This was necessary because following the institutionalisation of serfdom, along with the economic difficulties demesne lords faced, seignorial measures became more radical. Before they introduced higher burdens or forbade villagers from moving away, lords had to prove that villagers were indeed their serfs (which sometimes they could not do) [106]. Some Livonian villagers travelled all the way to Stockholm in the seventeenth century to address the high court and the king about their conflicts with demesne lords [98, 100].

Villagers were not easily intimidated and continued to resist stubbornly, although lords threatened them with or applied violence or ignored legal measures that were meant to protect the rural population. Even following small and comparatively harmless disagreements, tenants could be terrorised or robbed during violent raids and their property destroyed. Some or all resisters were thrown into prison to set an example. Protests could have serious repercussions, as in the case of Hans Rutenberg, who was evicted from his farm in the Brandenburg village of Woddow because he refused to render labour rents out of protest in 1692. Villagers of the estate of Wilsnack complained bitterly against the increased violence of their lord in pushing through his demands. They said that he behaved like a tyrant and even shot at some of them [40, 106, 123, 135]. The pain and humiliation of corporal punishment was often the target of villagers' protests [108]. Fugitives quoted fear and the experience of corporal punishment as one of the reasons for their escape [125]. Despite all their stubbornness and insubordination, villagers were only too aware that they had a lot to lose, hence they were, above all, cautious and far from united [124].

This shows that the level of everyday physical violence used to maintain the system should not be underestimated [43, 44, 116]. Beating servants and villagers during work was probably a widespread instrument of discipline. In this respect, too, the picture remains mixed. For instance, while on average 25 per cent of adult male serfs experienced corporal punishment on Russian noble estates, where labour rents prevailed in the late eighteenth and the first half of the nineteenth century, only 0.3 per cent suffered on *obrok* (quitrent) estates [45, 214, 223]. Within a system in which violence was a common instrument, little was sometimes required for an extreme eruption of violence to occur. Although it is fair to assume that on most occasions villagers were the victims, the anger of subjects and serfs could also easily turn against lords and particularly their representatives – mostly themselves from the rank of villagers [112]. While state authorities clearly took the side of the demesne lords in times of wider unrest, they also tried to intervene against excessive seignorial force and did punish lords for using it.

To summarise the 'view from the village' [115] in a nutshell, there was a lack of general economic destitution among villagers (see Chapter 5, Section iii) and the rural population were able to influence their fortunes to a surprising extent, either through cooperation with the seignorial regime or through insubordination and resistance against it. The situation is best exemplified by what was achieved by the village of Stolpe, near Berlin. On 15 December 1764, the whole village went to the administration of the royal estates located in Potsdam and suggested that they should take the village's demesne sheep farm on a hereditary lease for a rent of 220 *taler* per year. The inhabitants further indicated that they would be ready to receive their own farms, which they held in lease, in hereditary tenure, if the estate administration gave them the buildings and equipment for free. In other words, the people of Stolpe tried nothing less than to change the seignorial system in their village completely, abolishing demesne farming and receiving the full and hereditary property of their tenant farms. And they succeeded! The royal administration finally agreed to their proposal in 1769. The only condition was that the village made room for an additional four cottage households [149].

[vi]   Conclusions

The relationship between demesne lords and villagers must not be interpreted as serfdom on the part of the rural population. Many misinterpretations do in fact arise because of confusion about important differences in villagers' status and its meaning, even in the current literature. Regrettably, these contribute to the traditional image of a 'dualism' in European agrarian structures or a '(second) serfdom' in early modern East-Central and Eastern Europe. Given the regional variation all over Europe, these notions should be abandoned. To acknowledge the results of the new approaches to East-Central and Eastern European rural history would mean doing without the concept of a general serfdom and employing more useful concepts, like the English-language equivalents of terms in Czech, German, Hungarian, Polish or Slovak historiography such as demesne lordship. The system is now understood not as compact, but as including all the different manifestations of seignorialism in the area, which ranged from milder forms of lordship to serfdom, the latter limited to a small number of territories only.

   The actual practice of demesne lordship in individual regions and estates depended on the development of four main characteristics: mobility restrictions, jurisdictional powers of lords, property rights and labour rents (see Section iv). Variation in these characteristics largely explains the regional differences observed, which is why it is inadequate to think of demesne lordship as a monolithic system. This conclusion is largely owed to the most recent approaches, in which determined efforts to give priority to a view from the village highlighted the scope and possibilities of villagers and their institutions to influence and shape rural society. Demesne lordship, subjection and serfdom could interfere directly in several aspects of villagers' everyday lives. Yet many case studies illustrate that the power of demesne lords was far from absolute and that there were legal and other ways for successful action and resistance by the rural population. Villagers could and did determine their own affairs to a much larger degree than had previously been assumed. However, they often had to engage in bitter arguments and conflicts and incurred material losses to do so [210]. This suggests that there was continuous pressure from lords and – as everywhere else in Europe – from the growing power of the state. With the rise of state taxation, the military coercion of standing armies, the pressures of social discipline and confessional uniformity, it was hard for villagers to find their way anywhere in early modern Europe. Conflicts between them and the state or local authorities, therefore, should not sound entirely unfamiliar to students and scholars primarily concerned with the social and economic history of early modern Western and Southern Europe. It is this comparative perspective into which the analysis of East Elbian rural societies has to be placed.

3 Explaining the Rise of Demesne Lordship and the Demesne Economy

[i] Introduction

Research has long argued over an explanation for the rise of demesne lordship and about individual factors that influenced its establishment. A single explanatory approach has not yet been accepted, but the significance of influences such as the sixteenth-century price revolution or the political power yielded by the Estates is generally uncontested, even if disagreement arises as to their concrete effects and their importance relative to other factors. Various hypotheses have been proposed to explain the establishment of demesne lordship and the rise of the demesne economy. Possible explanations vary according to the theoretical approaches adopted. As discussed in Chapter 1, some favour analysis of the legal and political framework, while others give more weight to economic factors and particularly to what is regarded as the roughly simultaneous emergence of demesne lordship and a commercial demesne economy. This chapter will present a brief survey of explanations offered so far, then discuss and critically evaluate three approaches in greater detail.

[ii] Explaining the Establishment of Demesne Lordship

Explanatory approaches for the rise of demesne lordship frequently refer to elements outside the purely economic sphere. To begin with, the power of the nobility and Estates and the weakness of the state are conventionally regarded as important elements in explaining why lords were able to intensify their domination over villagers and establish a commercial demesne economy, which also built on extensive economic and trade privileges [45, 104]. According to the liberal reading, state interference in relations between demesne lords and villagers was to the benefit of the rural population (for instance in Brandenburg-Prussia or the Habsburg Monarchy). The particular political structure determined that noble lords were granted legal jurisdiction over their estates by the state – not only in minor matters, such as in local concerns and neighbourhood conflicts, but also with regard to high jurisdiction. The structure also helped to undermine the political and economic influence of towns or cities and caused their decline within an environment of generally low urbanisation [2, 104]. The lords used these powers to their advantage to shrug off the effects of the crisis of the late Middle Ages and price inflation. Lords in both East and West were confronted with the decline of feudal rents, but those in the East seem to have been more successful in shifting the burden of the crisis to villagers, because, as one theory summarised by Robert Brenner holds, the state and the rural population lacked the institutional means to prevent this 'refeudalisation' [1, 2, 22, 104]. Alternatively, the generally lower levels of population density and a high land/labour ratio are quoted as decisive factors in the lords' systematic shift to commercial demesne production in direct management, which also used labour rents [2, 45].

Critical issues regarding seignorial legal powers have already been discussed (see Chapter 2, Section iv). Demesne lordship and strong states thrived together, as Brandenburg-Prussia, the Habsburg Monarchy, Sweden or Russia would demonstrate [32, 33]. Regarding low urbanisation and the decline of towns, summary statistics based on the proportion of the population resident in cities of over 10 000 inhabitants indeed show that urbanisation in Eastern Europe lagged behind European averages by 1700 or 1800, whereas the gap had been much less pronounced in 1500. It seems straightforward to attribute low urbanisation to policies followed by the nobility in some territories of undermining town markets and gaining trade privileges at the expense of urban merchants. However, from a Central European perspective it may be inappropriate to classify urbanisation only on the basis of towns with a threshold of more than 10 000 inhabitants. Since the later Middle

41

Ages there had been a dense network of market and regional towns in the area that dominated the urban landscape. The usual approach also overlooks the growing significance of seignorial towns backed by their demesne lords, which precisely belonged to this group of towns below 5000 or 10 000 inhabitants. Including these, the urban population may have been between 20 and 30 per cent in the Czech Lands, Hungary, Great Poland or Royal Prussia [31, 61].

In an early modern context, assessing both urbanisation and population density would require consideration of regional rates rather than those based on the borders of modern nation states projected into the past. There were areas and territories in East-Central Europe in which there was a dense urban network and rates of urbanisation and population density were high, sometimes approaching Western European levels. Examples would be Lower Silesia, Upper Lusatia, Bohemia, Moravia, Royal Prussia and areas of Little Poland, let alone the European part of the Ottoman Empire (due to the exceptional size of Istanbul). It seems unlikely that regions around the many commercial and political urban centres in East-Central and Eastern Europe, such as the large Baltic trading ports, or Cracow, Poznań, Prague, Wrocław, the six free cities of Upper Lusatia and Berlin (after 1700), would not exert the same impact and offer the same commercial incentives as in the West of Europe [80, 83, 120, 178]. Looking at these areas also makes obvious the failure of the low urbanisation paradigm, as dynamic urban development could not generally prevent the occurrence of demesne lordship and of a demesne economy in these areas. In fact quite the opposite occurred: urban citizens, institutions and councils, especially of free territorial towns, themselves acquired considerable rural properties, in which they sometimes operated demesne farms with labour rents. What is more, these macro-level explanations operate in terms of the framework of a structural European dualism and disregard variations within countries due to the lack of comparative approaches.

Research established early a further factor to explain the rise of demesne lordship: the development of a commercial demesne economy [2, 52]. The labour demand from this economy was regarded as the reason for restricting the mobility of the rural population (see Chapter 2, Section iv) and for the rise of labour rents (see Chapter 4, Section iv). Returning to the effects of the late medieval crisis and sixteenth-century price inflation, it was the decline of seignorial income, widespread desertion of tenant farms, rising grain prices and a surge in demand due to sixteenth-century population growth in the West that led to demesne activities. In general, the literature distinguishes between the growth of demesnes related to export demand and those primarily related to domestic markets. For example, the issue of the significance of grain exports was taken up after 1945 with specific reference to Poland and the Baltic area.

[iii] Market and Export Demand

Among the territories that are usually associated with demesne lordship in one form or another, there were only two that can be considered as net importers of grain: Upper Lusatia and Silesia. All others were net exporters of grain or agricultural products to a varying extent, and would only fail to produce a surplus in exceptional periods such as extreme harvest failures or disruptions by war. It thus seems straightforward to assume that there must have been a connection between the rising grain demand of North-Western Europe beginning in the fifteenth century and the development of structures of demesne lordship in which lords operated large commercial estates, producing grain that was exported via Baltic ports, Hamburg or land routes.

The Polish economic historian Marian Małowist established the basic argument linking the early capitalist commercialisation of North-Western Europe in the fifteenth and sixteenth centuries with the rise of the demesne economy in the Baltic [28, 32, 33, 155, 160]. Fuelled by the sixteenth-century price revolution and price differences to Western Europe, the volume of grain exports from the Baltic rose significantly between the end of the fifteenth century and the eighteenth century, with peaks in the sixteenth and early seventeenth centuries. Gdańsk was the major export centre (see Table 3.1). This formed the empirical base of the hypothesis related to world system theories concerning a division of labour between Western and Eastern Europe, and represents an important pillar of macro-level theories of European economic development. According to world-systems theories, demesne lordship was not a result of Eastern European feudal structures, but the flip side of early capitalism in the European West – it was 'capitalist in origin' [28, 31, 47, 50, 160, 180].

Villagers and Lords in Eastern Europe, 1300–1800

Table 3.1 Rye, wheat and grain exports from Gdańsk, 1465–1656 (in 1000 *last*; 1562–5 to 1655–6 exports were through the Danish Sound originating from Gdańsk)

Year	Rye	Wheat	Grain (total)
1465	2.3	–	–
1470	2.2	–	–
1490	9.5	–	–
1492	10.2	–	–
1530	14.0	–	–
1557	21.0–29.0	–	40.5
1562–65	42.7	4.8	52.5
1566–69	35.4	2.3	37.9
1574–79	19.8	2.1	27.8
1580–84	18.9	2.6	22.9
1585–89	27.4	2.7	30.6
1590–94	27.1	1.8	29.5
1595–99	38.1	4.6	43.3
1600–04	–	–	33.8
1605–09	–	–	44.5
1610–14	–	–	36.5
1615–19	–	–	50.9
1620–24	–	–	45.8
1625–26	–	–	24.8
1630–33	–	–	23.9
1635–39	–	–	40.3
1640–44	–	–	69.1
1645–49	–	–	45.2
1650–54	–	–	16.2
1655–56	–	–	26.4

Note: 1 *last* = approx. 2.2 tons; 1562–65 to 1655–66 annual averages.
Sources: [55, 57, 59, 62].

There is mixed evidence as to the significance of grain and other agricultural exports from the Eastern Baltic ports such as Kaliningrad, Tallinn and Riga, and the degree of involvement of demesne farming in this area. Livonian landlords seem to have developed an interest in grain exports in the early sixteenth century, but other goods such as flax and hemp (not only from demesne production), timber or potash may have played a greater role in the export than in Gdańsk. In Tallinn, only 50 per cent of exports were

44

grain; in Riga grain formed about one third in the seventeenth and eighteenth centuries (and roughly two-thirds were flax and hemp). With 10–15 000 *last* of grain shipped annually in the first half of the seventeenth century, exports from these ports together also represented a rather small proportion of that sent out of Gdańsk. During the late seventeenth century, grain exports from Riga, Tallinn, Pärnu and others increased and export of grain gained a larger share of total exports and of grain production in these countries [93, 98, 100, 101]. For Russia, grain exports during the sixteenth century seem unlikely, as in 1702 their value was only 2 per cent of total exports. Such exports reached more significant levels only after 1760 [222].

The role of exports has also been discussed in relation to Mecklenburg, Pomerania and Brandenburg. The prince's interference in Dutch grain exports from Wismar and Rostock illustrates that grain was exported from Mecklenburg around 1500 [32, 123]. There is little information about the quantities exported, however. Szczecin was an important grain export harbour for Pomerania and parts of Brandenburg [145]. Regular Brandenburg grain exports between the fourteenth century and 1600 may have collapsed in the first half of the seventeenth century under the impact of the Thirty Years' War. As in the Eastern Baltic and Poland, lords secured trade privileges for grain exports. Based on 1563–4 customs data from the port of Lenzen on the river Elbe, Hartmut Harnisch estimates that about 9000 tons of grain were exported from the western parts of the Brandenburg Kurmark annually. In addition, grain from the eastern districts of Uckermark and Barnim was usually hauled via Szczecin, in the 1580s at quantities of about 3000 tons per year. In total, 10–15 000 tons of grain may have been exported every year between 1560 and 1620 [119, 123]. Domestic grain markets as well as land exports to neighbouring territories such as Saxony also played a role in grain demand and demesne farming. The recovery of the population after the Thirty Years' War, the growth of urban centres and the incorporation of industrial provinces such as Silesia may have increased the importance of domestic markets relative to grain exports in Brandenburg in this period [118].

The Kingdom of Hungary forms a special case within the 'export demand' hypothesis, because its main export goods in the sixteenth and seventeenth centuries were cattle, copper and wine. Hungarian grain exports were relatively negligible given the country's landlocked position, but grain production in the sixteenth century was stimulated by domestic markets due to necessary supplies during the wars between the Habsburg and Ottoman Empires [153, 155, 159]. Particularly in regions closer to the western border, large-scale demesne farms did evolve during the sixteenth century. However, only well into the eighteenth century did lords systematically turn again to demesne arable farming and the country became a significant exporter of grain after 1750 [153, 155]. In 1767, grain had reached second place by value among exports (16 per cent) [58].

Wine was probably a more important export good. Nevertheless, it was not necessarily primarily produced by demesnes, but bought from tenants or collected as rent. The quantity exported amounted to about 100–110 000 hectolitres per annum (10–15 per cent of Hungarian wine production) in the sixteenth and seventeenth centuries [154]. Livestock was the main export in this period. While about 50 000 oxen were exported from Hungary in 1562 via different routes to Venice, Austria and particularly Southern Germany, the number reached 130 000 in 1587 and maybe even 200 000 in peak years until 1600. The annual average was about 100 000 heads in 1550–1600 and 60 000 in 1600–50. The value represented about 75 per cent of total export in 1550–1600 and 45 per cent in 1600–50 [58, 153, 154, 155, 159]. In 1767, livestock was still the top export good, although its share had declined to 27.1 per cent [58].

Denmark, Schleswig-Holstein and the Ukraine (Podolia, Ruthenia), Moldavia and Walachia were further centres for livestock exports. Around 1600, the Duchy of Schleswig was dependent on imports of rye, but specialised in exports of barley, cheese and oxen. Danish grain accounted for 10 per cent of total Baltic grain exports in 1600. Livestock exports from Denmark became significant as early as the fifteenth century and in the peak year 1612, more than 100 000 heads were exported from Denmark and Schleswig-Holstein over land (on average 45–50 000 in 1540–80 and 55–60 000 in 1600–20, while after 1650 only 20–30 000 was the rule). Some 30–60 000 heads per year came from Eastern Poland, the Ukraine and the South East of Europe. By contrast, the possibility of grain exports seemed to have a pronounced influence on the extension of demesne farming in Scania [28, 47, 91, 92, 160]. There were considerable grain and sheep exports from Romania and Wallachia to the centres of the Ottoman Empire during the early modern period; in the eighteenth century this region was seen as a major export centre. Lords took much of these exports from the surplus of tenant farmers. At the end of the eighteenth century, an estimated 200–300 000 sheep were exported to Istanbul each year [14, 47, 134, 154, 164].

While there is evidence that considerable amounts of grain were exported from the Baltic to North-Western Europe from the late fifteenth century onwards (Table 3.1) and that the demesne economy profited from this demand, it seems not without problems to conclude that this had a general impact on all regions and territories in Eastern Europe. Even for Poland, which presented the classic case for this theory, it is highly unlikely that landlocked estates not situated close to navigable rivers, such as in Little Poland, Red Ruthenia, Podolia or the Grand Duchy of Lithuania, would produce exports for the Baltic. During the second half of the sixteenth century, the majority of the grain exported from Gdańsk still came from the surrounding regions of Royal Prussia, Cuiavia, Eastern Great Poland and from areas of Mazovia. Only when prices picked up around 1550 did rye and wheat from Podlasia along the rivers of Bug and Narew and from Little Poland and Ruthenia increasingly appear on the Gdańsk market [164, 179]. Urbanisation rates varied in Poland, which meant that domestic markets played a greater role in certain regions.

At a greater distance from Gdańsk, only the largest estates would be able to sell grain at a profit to the export cities. Consequently, in Little Poland and Red Ruthenia Polish magnates participated in the grain trade to Gdańsk, and they came to dominate over time as grain prices fell after their peak around 1600. While only between a quarter and a third of the grain at the Włocławek customs came from estates of magnates in Mazovia in 1555–76 (and about a quarter from those of the gentry), the magnates' share of the grain shipped from Little Poland and Ruthenia was between 57 and 70 per cent [179]. In total, the share of nobles in providing grain for export via Gdańsk is estimated at around 70 per cent for the period around 1600 [160, 180].

Contrary to the reasoning of the 'export hypothesis', Cuiavia and Mazovia were the regions in which the demesne economy was less developed than elsewhere in Poland. The inland regions of Little Poland and Western Poland had a higher proportion of demesne land (as a percentage of total land; see Table 4.1) than Mazovia, from where more than 40 per cent of the grain at the Włocławek customs originated in the late sixteenth century. Estimates of regional differences in labour rents in that period do not show unanimous support for the 'export hypothesis' either. For instance, in Eastern Great Poland the majority of demesnes were run without forced labour, despite the link to export markets (see Table 4.9) [180, 206].

Polish economic historians also drew attention to the rather limited weight of exports in relation to total demesne and tenant grain production (estimated at c.1.37 million tons net of seed for the 1560s and 1570s, of which 0.6 million tons were rye and 0.17 million wheat; and 1.47 million tons for 1580, of which 0.97 million were rye and 0.12 million wheat) [198, 200]. While estimated at only 2.5 to 4 per cent of gross production in the sixteenth century (and 9.3 per cent of rye production), export share may have risen to between 7 and 16 per cent of total grain production in 1600–49. This would represent 17 to 36 per cent of gross rye production and suggests an important, but not dominant impact. Other historians pointed to the fact that exports have to be measured against the volumes of grain entering the market, for instance representing up to 40 per cent of the rye marketed during the sixteenth century). The decisive factor for the rise of demesne farming thus seems to have been the growth of markets for agricultural products in general; that is, including domestic markets. The role of the latter may have been underestimated by macro-level theories of a European division of labour [64, 160, 180, 190, 198].

If exports and European market integration were decisive factors, this would rule out the existence of a demesne economy in regions unaffected by grain exports, which cannot be reconciled with the regional distribution of demesne lordship and the demesne economy. An export orientation for sixteenth-century demesne farming is explicitly refuted for Hungary, Upper Lusatia and Lower Silesia. Although demesne lords and tenant farmers exported grain in considerable quantities from Bohemia, particularly along the river Elbe or over land routes to Saxony, the export trade was never regarded as a decisive reason for the growth of the demesne economy in Bohemia and Moravia either [47, 55, 80]. It was first and foremost the integration of domestic markets that fuelled demesne growth in eighteenth-century Russia.

[iv]   The Consequences of the Thirty Years' War

Another traditional approach to explain the growth of the demesne economy proposes an entirely different chronology and thus fundamentally questions the 'export demand' hypothesis. According to this view, the rise of a demesne economy based on labour rents was the result of the consequences of the Thirty Years' War and the demographic crisis of the seventeenth century.

Even for territories in which the situation of villagers is sometimes regarded as weak in the period before 1600, such as in Mecklenburg, Western and Eastern Pomerania or Poland, the literature identifies a further deterioration of their rights and considerable increase of labour rents during the seventeenth century. The major explanation seems to lie in the lack of available labour, which resulted from the widespread disruption, desertion, migration and epidemics caused by the Thirty Years' War and the Northern Wars. The demesne economy faced shrinking demand, falling grain prices and rising wages for agricultural labour. In this secular crisis of profit, the lords put into practice the privileges they had acquired with the backing of territorial rulers since the sixteenth century. This reasoning is to some extent based on the chronological coincidence of major territorial law codes passed roughly within the period 1620 to 1690, which repeat and reinforce measures about mobility restrictions, the downgrading of tenant property rights, forced service, seignorial market privileges and in a minority of territories even the established personal serfdom of the rural population (see Chapter 2, Section i) [20, 22, 123, 128, 160, 170], although this is not necessarily causal. This theory was particularly applied to the establishment of the demesne economy in Bohemia and Moravia and has re-emerged in recent scholarship [66, 76]. Although demesne operations expanded during the sixteenth century as elsewhere, researchers maintain that they were run largely without labour rents before 1620 [20, 55, 67, 76, 80].

Hartmut Harnisch and William Hagen present forceful rejections of the 'Thirty Years' War hypothesis' for Brandenburg. To Harnisch, the rise of demesne lordship and of the demesne economy was complete by 1600–20. Even before 1600, demesne farming was the dominant factor in landlords' income, the majority of demesne farms were run with labour rents to some degree, and legislation to restrict the mobility of the rural population and force young adults into seignorial agricultural service was already in place [17, 119]. Economic incentives for an extension of demesnes were also far stronger before 1620–50 than after, when grain prices were low and demand shrank [17].

William Hagen's research confirms and extends this account. The lords had massively lost in authority due to the upheaval caused by the war, aggravated by additional wars in the 1650s and 1670s [114]. Some were driven into ruin, others had to establish themselves in estates that were heavily depopulated and lacked operating tenant farms and manpower. As wage levels were high, grain prices low and export markets lost, demesne farming was barely profitable. Many indebted estates were sold or pledged, sometimes to town citizens with the necessary investment capital, but also to wealthy tenant farmers [106]. Although there were attempts to re-establish the pre-war order of demesne lordship with the help of the absolutist state in the 1650s [106, 123, 135], the exactions of landlords had to compete with those of the state (a 'post-war crisis in distribution'). Bargaining power was on the side of the villagers, who had to be attracted, for example by lower rents, to take over vacant holdings and render rents and labour. Until the late seventeenth century, lords in Brandenburg were largely unsuccessful in tightening demesne lordship any further. Villagers stepped up their resistance against attempts to increase exactions in this situation [123]. Given this situation and the lack of investment capital, demesne lords often opted for a cheap solution and began large-scale sheep farming on deserted land or ruined demesnes, which did not cause any additional burdens on the remaining tenants. Arable demesne farms had to be operated with wage labour, because the necessary labour rents were not available and burdens could not be increased [106, 114, 135]. This also had consequences for the further development of social relations after the demographic and economic recovery, when villagers met increasing landlord demands with resistance and were partly supported by the powerful legal institutions of the Brandenburg absolutist state, which was primarily interested in maintaining taxation levels. Rather than strengthening the position of demesne lords, the war had a weakening effect, as might be expected given the shift of bargaining power towards the rural population due to the demographic and economic crisis.

By analogy, these results cast doubt on whether lords in other territories could really succeed in suppressing the interests of villagers even more after 1650 than before. For instance, despite a further growth of demesne land at the expense of tenant land in Mecklenburg, lords were actually in a weaker bargaining position than before the war [128]. They needed to find tenants to operate farms left vacant due to desertions and population scarcity and to equip these farms, because villagers could not raise the necessary capital. Villagers were offered incentives to take over a holding, but even if this reduced their tenure to a leasehold of limited duration, it is difficult to imagine that anybody would be willing to take over an abandoned farm without being able to negotiate the level of rents at least to some extent. That the re-occupation of tenant holdings after the war had some priority in Mecklenburg can also be seen in the rising number of tenant farmers until 1700, even if it did not reach pre-war levels. Tenant farmers could easily lease additional land after desertions and the largest farms, those of the hereditary village headmen, made particular use of this development. Often new tenants came from other regions and therefore they were formally free and not the lord's subjects. Not least because of tenant resistance, lords had to wait for a stabilisation of the economy in the 1690s before they tried to increase labour rents any further. Tenants also challenged seignorial attempts to seize some of their land by petitioning the duke. Nevertheless, lords could and did exploit weaker tenant property rights to their advantage. For instance, when tenant farms were rebuilt by new tenants, demesne lords in Pomerania took these for their demesne farms and made the tenants take over another deserted farmholding [128].

In the case of the Czech Lands, recent studies emphasise the significance of the long-term position, re-aligning the analysis of developments in these territories with those of others in East-Central Europe. It is clear that regional differences prevailed with regard to the use of labour rents and the significance of the demesne economy during the sixteenth century, but such differences did not disappear after 1650 when it was claimed that demesne lordship took full hold. There is enough empirical evidence to show that on many estates, demesne farming relied heavily on *corvée* and mobility restrictions were in place before 1620 [5, 42]. Whether lords could really step up the pressure after 1620–50 with immediate success seems doubtful, as they had to compete with higher state taxation and were also confronted with a better bargaining position of villagers, particularly in areas devastated by war and emigration. This became obvious in case studies demonstrating that lords tolerated tenant debts, granted help to rebuild farms and smallholdings, and offered rent-free years or rent reductions (for labour rents as well) [72, 85].

Similar problems of an alleged post-1650 strengthening of demesne lordship may be assumed for the Baltic. The Great Northern War, a famine in 1697 and a plague in 1710–11 caused desertions and population decline in Estonia and Livonia. The remaining tenants were of great value to landlords, so obligations were lowered (or owed for some time) and tenants were able to cultivate deserted land in addition to their farms if they had enough manpower. New tenants were attracted with special conditions, such as rent-free years. As late as 1758, observers commented on the availability of deserted land. Only later in the eighteenth century, when the economy and population had recovered, did landlord pressure increase again, partly fuelled by the possibility of agricultural exports to Russia [94, 95, 96, 100].

A comparative view casts doubt on the causality supporting the traditional hypothesis about the effects of the seventeenth-century crisis in strengthening demesne lordship [20, 160]. The conditions of a lack of labour due to demographic decline or migration, which is held responsible for higher wages and consequently a shift towards higher labour rents, did not occur everywhere. The hypothesis is also at odds with explanations that rely on long-term developments since the later Middle Ages (see Sections iii and v). Between 1400–50 and 1620, almost all the regulations that made possible the establishment of hereditary subjection or serfdom of the rural population, such as lords' acquisition of legal powers or mobility restrictions, were put in place throughout East-Central and Eastern Europe. The process of increasing labour rents had also already started in the fifteenth and sixteenth centuries (see Chapter 4, Section iv) [2, 36]. This hypothesis relies on a chronology of the establishment of demesne lordship and the widespread imposition of labour rents for the demesne economy that cannot be reconciled with explanations referring to the significance for this process of secular trends in the European agrarian economy and the sixteenth-century price revolution [17].

[v] Medieval Continuities

Several research traditions claim that early modern developments in rural East-Central and Eastern Europe were rooted in settlement and power structures formed in the Middle Ages. According to such research, they can thus only be explained by a long-term perspective including the later Middle Ages. This approach has two variants. The first regards as paramount the formation of certain legal and constitutional structures, in particular a concentration of powers in the hands of the lords [22, 30]; however, the description often remains vague and lacks references to empirical case studies. The second variant attributes social and economic changes to the effects of the crisis of the late Middle Ages and its desertions, population migration or losses and structural decline of feudal rent income. Though the crisis had an almost universal impact in Europe, there were different consequences for East and West [1, 4, 48, 56]. Various authors have argued that in East-Central and Eastern Europe lords succeeded in transferring the burdens of the economic consequences to the rural population. This was due to specific social property relations, the lack of protection offered by the emerging state against the advances of lords and a lack of cohesion among village communities to enable them to resist successfully. In order to react to the secular decline of income due to inflation of the value of customary cash rents and a lack of tenants, lords in East-Central and Eastern Europe turned to a commercial demesne economy [1, 2, 22, 49, 115, 119].

The general applicability of such reasoning breaks down in the light of more recent research, however. Empirical studies on Bohemia, Brandenburg, Western Pomerania and Lower Silesia have shown that there were major discontinuities in the development of demesne lordship and the demesne economy between the late fourteenth and sixteenth centuries. These contradict traditional suggestions that the special agrarian structure of demesne lordship was already embedded in the organisation of late medieval rural society and economy. In addition, the traditional contrast of exaggerating villagers' rights in the later Middle Ages and lamenting their deterioration afterwards seems to misrepresent both late medieval and early modern conditions for purely teleological reasons [9].

Despite the fact that demesne farms were widespread in East-Central Europe in the later Middle Ages, there seems to have been no direct continuity between the farms and the commercial demesne economy after 1500. For the Lower Silesian Duchy of Wrocław, Richard Hoffmann demonstrated fragmentation of estate ownership and the alternation of strong shifts towards demesne farming on the one hand and abandoning demesnes on the other between the thirteenth and early sixteenth centuries [169]. Property turnover, fragmentation of noble land ownership and estate discontinuity were high in areas of Brandenburg before the consolidation of the demesne economy during the sixteenth century. Only about 15 per cent of the noble families in the district of Uckermark held their estate property continuously from before 1400 until after 1500 [106]. The estate of Boitzenburg became one of the largest noble estates in Brandenburg in the 1520s and 1530s, but in 1375 the 16 villages were still split among 33 different lords [118]. In Brandenburg only about 25–30 per cent of the early modern demesne farms existed in 1375 and only 20 per cent of the demesne farmland in 1800 was directly managed by 1375 [22, 106]. In Brandenburg and Mecklenburg, medieval demesne farms were small and not really oriented towards market production. Demesne development in Bohemia was also marked by major discontinuities in the fifteenth century [65].

The observable increase in demesne land in some parts of Brandenburg or in the Duchy of Wrocław in the late fourteenth and fifteenth centuries are not seen as a result of an early systematic attempt to install a commercialized demesne economy, but rather as a halt to further conversion of demesnes into rental land or an emergency reaction to maintain cultivation in the face of population decline, lack of tenants and agricultural recession [106, 169]. In Eastern Pomerania, the continuous existence of individual medieval demesne farms is not regarded as a precondition to the sixteenth-century expansion of demesne farming [192]. In Eastern Holstein, where many demesne farms were already established during the medieval settlement period, the process of consolidating and relocating these farms prior to the full development of a commercially oriented demesne economy lasted at least until well into the sixteenth century [134, 136, 137].

The view that medieval conditions caused a lack of cohesion in village communities and helped demesne lords to downgrade their functions as institutions and the role of their representatives during the early modern period has also been challenged in recent research (see Chapter 2, Section v). Village communities maintained medieval rights and legal and administrative functions and continued to exist as relevant institutions [71, 85, 107]. Negotiations about rents, tenant and communal land and especially about the introduction of labour rents show that villagers could resist seignorial moves or decisively influence the conditions under which changes were implemented (see Chapter 4, Section iv).

Despite these obvious problems of the general hypothesis of late medieval continuities, recent studies shed light on the long-term impact that late medieval developments may have had. In Little Poland, the establishment of a demesne economy could indeed have had a late medieval basis under particular conditions. During the fourteenth and fifteenth centuries, individual demesne farms were extended and concentrated in the central parts of feudal estates, while smaller ones were abandoned and their land redistributed to tenants. Existing farms were worked with labour rents. The change was most visible in large church properties, which traditionally kept close market links because of the significant quantities of tithe grain they received. In a more limited way, noble estates, for instance in the vicinity of the Cracow market, also followed this development. Market connections seem to have been crucial, because in other, more remote regions the feudal economy continued on a pure rent basis, in which demesne farms were maintained only for reasons of supply for local noble households [163]. This points to an influence of medieval continuities in particular regional contexts. As a more general trend, affecting also the smaller estates of the lower nobility, the rise in demesne farming was a reaction to the crisis of the tenant economy and increasing desertions. In this case, the development began in the late fifteenth and early sixteenth centuries. The crisis specifically affected regions in which tenant agriculture was not well connected to markets [163].

In Mecklenburg, too, certain elements point to the relevance of long-term continuities for building demesnes. The majority of the large landed estates of the nobility in the sixteenth and seventeenth centuries were held by the oldest aristocratic families in the country. The centres of their demesne economy can be traced to the original medieval centres of estate administration [131]. Similar observations have also been made for certain regions of Western Pomerania and await further empirical clarification [145]. In Schleswig-Holstein, the desertions of the later Middle Ages may have helped church and noble lords to extend and consolidate their medieval demesnes [136, 137]. In certain regions and territories, therefore, the continuity of noble estate ownership may have made possible a long-term process of change towards a commercial demesne economy.

Further possible support for the importance of long-term changes since the Middle Ages comes from an approach recently formulated by Tom Scott, which regards the growth of demesne lordship as a gradual process of concentration of lordship powers. This seems to make it necessary to differentiate analytically between these processes and the (later) rise of the demesne economy. Accordingly, Scott argues that '(t)he rise of *Gutsherrschaften* [demesne lordship] preceded – by as much as three centuries in some cases – the emergence of *Gutswirtschaften* [demesne economy]' [69]. On this basis, the long-term effects of changes in the late medieval period can be meaningfully analysed with reference to their regional contexts and their specific relevance to selected aspects of demesne lordship [5]. The approach thus seems promising for future research. By means of a differentiated analysis, it avoids the false assumption that late medieval agrarian structures automatically predetermined the rise of early modern demesne lordship.

[vi] Conclusions

Existing theories to explain the rise of early modern demesne lordship and its most significant element, the commercial demesne economy, suffer from the problem that they were developed on the basis of studies that investigated only developments in particular countries and were later applied to a more general context. Consequently, any analysis more systematically based on a comparative perspective will highlight shortcomings and deviations and will not find the standard explanations satisfactory. A comparative approach was chosen in this chapter to criticise the arguments of theories that explain the establishment of the demesne economy in terms of the sixteenth-century growth of export markets or the seventeenth-century crisis. While the export factor was probably weaker than assumed or missing altogether for several regions and territories, explanations based on the impact of ruptures like wars or the crisis of the seventeenth century fail to consider long-term changes that formed the basis for developments after 1600. They seem to exaggerate seignorial powers in the face of demographic crisis and the rise of the absolutist tax state.

The idea of a structural difference between Western and Eastern Europe should be treated with extreme caution, in particular with respect to possible medieval roots. Some of the general trends influencing the tenant economy in late medieval Western Europe – such as the fragmentation of lordship, the reduction of demesne farming, urbanisation and changes in property rights and tenure – also occurred in East-Central and Eastern Europe. The concrete impact of these changes, which requires further analysis, was potentially as favourable for economic development in general and tenant farming in particular as in the West. The flaws of the conventional theory of medieval continuities of demesne lordship, which became obvious due to recent empirical studies, clearly demonstrate that it cannot form a satisfactory explanation for the changes in seignorial relations and the establishment of the demesne economy without major revisions. In particular, arguments about the medieval agrarian constitution predetermining rural development in East-Central and Eastern Europe, or any other form of general determinism, need to be reflected. Recent studies, concentrating on specific aspects and regions rather than imposing a general continuity, provide some justification for analysing the consequences of the crisis of the later Middle Ages in terms of its long-term effects on the development of the rural society and economy. These demonstrated with respect to examples in Brandenburg, the Czech Lands and Poland that an analysis of late medieval structures can indeed offer insights into the genesis of later trends in development and point to the gradual nature of the change towards the establishment of demesne lordship and a commercial demesne economy. A promising approach seems to be to separate analytically the development of demesne lordship from that of a commercial demesne economy. This approach needs to be based on a new understanding of demesne lordship and its consequences for the rural population, as outlined in Chapter 2. The results of recent case studies on Brandenburg, the Czech Lands, Mecklenburg or Poland help to trace how developments beginning in the later Middle Ages influenced the significant processes during the sixteenth century that formed decisive steps towards demesne lordship and the demesne economy.

4 A Fresh Characterisation of the Demesne Economic System

[i]   Introduction

An extensive and commercially oriented demesne economy formed the economic basis of demesne lordship. It was established from the sixteenth century onwards, but with quite varying densities, and differences occurred in the relative importance of arable demesne farming and other sectors of the demesne economy. Several approaches to demesne lordship agree that its rise caused the most important economic consequences for the development of the tenant economy because of the possible seizure of tenant land, the reliance on tenant labour rents and possible competition for its products on local and international markets. This chapter will investigate the economic structure in detail by analysing the extent of demesne farming and its variation over time, the sectors of the demesne economy and their importance for seignorial income, as well as the extent of labour rents and the processes that led to their establishment. It will challenge generalisations in the literature and earlier descriptions such as that labour rents could simply be imposed on villagers, that demesne farms were predominantly operated with forced labour and that lords simply seized tenant land to extend their demesnes.

[ii]   The Myth of the Expropriation of Tenant Farmers

For some time the conviction prevailed that the extension of demesne farming occurred at the expense of tenant land. According to this reasoning, from the late fifteenth century onwards thousands of tenant farmers were denied their property rights and were expelled from their holdings – sometimes with compensation, sometimes without – and their land was seized to build new demesne farms, the production on which was geared to supra-regional or export markets. This development was called *Bauernlegen* (literally, removing tenant farmers). The survey of tenant property rights (see Chapter 2, Section iv) has already indicated that the image of a general expropriation of East-Central and Eastern European tenant farmers and smallholders is mistaken. There is a need to differentiate between expropriations and other conflicts about resources, such as agricultural waste, deserted land, common pasture, forests, rivers, lakes and ponds, which lords began to claim more systematically for their own use in the fifteenth and sixteenth centuries to exploit them more intensively or expand directly managed farms or animal husbandry. Often lacking formal proof of their use rights, villagers were frequently unable to prevent lords from seizing these areas.

In territories in which tenant property rights remained secure, the extension of demesne into tenant land was possible only if villagers were willing to sell their holdings or if the land was deserted. Individual abuses occurred everywhere, but villagers would not hesitate to set in motion legal procedures to defend their rights. Certainly by the eighteenth century, expropriation of hereditary tenures without compensation was very difficult indeed, and only had a chance of succeeding if lords could prove that tenants had failed to deliver payments or mismanaged their holdings.

This general framework aside, the seizure of tenant farmland could still be substantial in certain cases. The Duchy of Mecklenburg is an extreme example, where tenant property rights gradually eroded between 1573 and 1621 [128]. Developments were quite similar in Eastern Pomerania where in 1556 noble landlords received the right to seize tenant holdings as long as tenants were compensated. The formal abolition of tenant property rights occurred in 1616 and became valid in Western Pomerania in 1645. The particularly strong position of the Estates vis-à-vis the prince in Mecklenburg and (Western) Pomerania meant that expropriations were sanctioned on such a large scale and continued during the eighteenth century, contrary to the opposite tendency in most other territories [123, 145]. In the eastern parts of the Duchies of Schleswig and

Holstein, farmers were already regarded as leaseholders at will in the later Middle Ages and expropriations occurred at a greater scale in the early modern period [126, 139].

In these countries, expropriation of tenant farms occurred primarily on estates owned by the nobility. In Mecklenburg there were 25 000 tenant farmers in 1628. About 12–14 000 belonged to noble estates, and their number decreased to 4900 in 1755 [22, 133]. As a result of the introduction of new farming techniques (see Chapter 5, Section ii), many of the remaining full tenant farmholdings in noble estates were seized after 1700, and farmers were forced to earn their livelihood as cottagers and day labourers for the remaining tenant and demesne farms. The peak of expropriation was reached between 1750 and 1820. Quite a different policy was followed on princely estates, where expropriations did not occur or tenants were relocated to new farms elsewhere. The number of tenant farms on princely estates barely shrank [22, 128].

From a more general perspective, the extension of demesne farmland did not usually rely on expelling tenants from their farms. First, during the sixteenth century land abandoned towards the end of the Middle Ages was put back into use by extending demesnes. Secondly, lords also established demesnes following later desertions such as after the Thirty Years' War or the Northern Wars. Thirdly, in most areas there were important land reserves or uninhabited land and forests that could be used.

The case of Western Pomerania, where tenant property rights were undermined in a similar manner as in Mecklenburg, illustrates well that the growth of demesne farms between 1560 and 1610 was based on a combination of these mechanisms. In the initial stages, lords partly bought the farms of their tenants or compensated them with land elsewhere. It is of course difficult to judge whether they always received market prices and how much force was used to 'convince' them to sell, but documents in Western Pomerania as well as in other territories suggest that considerable sums were paid for some holdings. In individual noble estates all of the taxable tenant hides had been expropriated between 1580 and 1597, whereas in others their numbers hardly changed. In the seventeenth and eighteenth centuries expropriations continued in Western Pomerania [144]. The remaining tenant farmholdings on noble estates had largely disappeared by 1800 [22, 145]. In some regions of Eastern Pomerania seizing tenant land seems to have been more important, but especially in the first quarter of the sixteenth century there were still abundant land reserves to prevent extensive expropriations during the initial phases of demesne growth [192].

In most of East-Central and Eastern Europe, expropriations were unknown on such a scale. Demesne lords could not simply seize tenant land, but had to follow legal procedures and regulations. For instance in Brandenburg, lords received legal permission to buy tenant farmland or to seize deserted tenant farms in 1536 and the right to purchase tenant farms under certain conditions in 1540. There were generally enough land reserves and desertions to prevent large-scale expropriation, which is why the number of occupied tenant farms and smallholdings actually increased during the sixteenth century [17]. In the Middle Mark, 45.9 per cent of demesne farmland in 1800 (and as much as 75.1 per cent in the district of Uckermark) came from desertions. Between 1575 and 1624, a period of major demesne expansion, the nobility seized less than 10 per cent of the total available tenant farmland [22, 115].

The extension of demesne farms in the Czech Lands, Hungary and Poland between the sixteenth and eighteenth centuries was not based on systematic expropriations either. In Hungary, the incidence of expropriation is estimated at less than 1.5 per cent of tenant land, reaching up to 10 per cent only in areas in which arable land was scarcer [155]. In other territories there were no instances of seizing tenant land on a mass scale.

[iii]   The Expansion and Extent of Demesne Farming

The macro-economic framework of rising grain prices during the sixteenth and early seventeenth centuries determined some characteristics common to the building of the demesne economy throughout East-Central Europe, despite important differences between individual territories. The proportion of demesne land varied enormously both regionally and over time. Systematic differences occurred for instance between noble estates and those held by other lords (princely, crown and town or church institutions). The aggregate estimates, which were computed for whole territories or provinces mostly on the basis of tax surveys, can only be a very rough guide (see Tables 4.1–4.8).

In Poland, there was a considerable increase of demesne land from the first half of the sixteenth century. The proportion of demesne land was typically higher on noble estates than on church and crown ones, but there was also considerable variation in the density of demesne farms in individual regions. In 1600, demesne and tenant land reached parity and by 1630 demesnes covered a larger area than tenant holdings in Great Poland (Table 4.1) [28, 174]. Depending on the extent of desertions of tenant farms in the seventeenth century, the share of demesne land could increase further. For instance, in the districts of Korczyn and Sandomierz the proportion of demesne land increased strongly until 1660 (when it almost reached parity with tenant land in Sandomierz, while in 1611 demesnes only held 20 per cent of the total) because many tenant holdings were vacant. In Korczyn, demesne area was reduced by half between 1572 and 1660 and nevertheless the share compared to tenant land increased from 1 to 3.1 to 1 to 2.3 [170, 181, 189, 199].

In contrast, tenant farming dominated in Royal Prussia. For example, demesne share of land was only 26 per cent in the voivodship of Chełmno in the late sixteenth century. In royal estates in the Cracow area, seignorial land was primarily made up of forests and the share of demesne arable land could be as small as 5 per cent as late as the second half of the eighteenth century [161, 165, 172, 176]. The structure of individual estates in Belorussia and the Grand Duchy of Lithuania suggests that demesnes comprised a much smaller share of the land in these regions in the seventeenth and eighteenth centuries. The eastern parts of the country were

Table 4.1 Proportion of noble demesne and tenant land, Poland c.1600 (%)

Region	Demesne land	Tenant land
Eastern Great Poland	50	50
Little Poland	45	55
Western Great Poland	44	56
Mazovia	40	60
All regions	44	56

Source: [197].

far from commercial centres and ports, hence demesne density was low. Demesnes seemed to have been of relatively small importance for income in princely estates of the Grand Duchy. As a reaction to general circumstances, the number of demesnes even declined until the middle of the eighteenth century [172, 188]. In Lithuanian royal estates there was an ambitious re-introduction of demesne farming in the late 1760s that yielded high profits [29].

Demesne farming expanded in Mecklenburg during the sixteenth century and the widespread desertions after 1650 further increased its share. In early eighteenth-century Mecklenburg-Schwerin, the intensity of demesne farming was much stronger on noble estates. There were also important regional differences in the density of demesne farms between the north and the south of the Duchy. An overall estimate for the size of demesne land on noble estates suggests a third of the total in 1635; by 1700 the share had grown to about 52 per cent [143].

In the princely and noble estates of Pomerania, the period between 1560 and the beginning of the Thirty Years' War was marked by a strong increase in the number of demesne farms [145, 192]. A 1692–8 survey of 1103 villages shows that demesnes covered 59 per cent of the total land. This is an extraordinary proportion even among territories of demesne lordship [144]. Table 4.2 suggests that demesne farming in Western Pomerania had already reached a considerable size by the beginning of the Thirty Years' War.

In noble estates in the south-east of Schleswig-Holstein, between 51 and 59 per cent of the arable area was demesne land. Demesnes also arose on princely and noble estates in the northern and central districts of the country between 1550 and 1600. The first stagnation began in the 1590s, when the princely administration dissolved some of the demesnes for economic reasons. Together with a systematic conversion of labour services into cash rents between 1630 and 1660, this led to an abandonment of demesnes in most of the country's north [136, 140]. For the regions of demesne lordship in Schleswig, the ratio of demesne to tenant land was about 1:1 by 1700, in east Holstein the ratio was 1:1 in 1652 and demesne land exceeded that of tenants by 1700 [134]. Elsewhere in Denmark such an expansion did not occur. Demesne farming expanded between 1525 and 1699, particularly after 1630 when 319 new farms were built, while 184 were abandoned in the same period. Rising state pressure for taxes from the rural population made it difficult for

Table 4.2 Ratio between demesne and tenant land, selected estates in Western Pomerania, 1556–1631 (in number of hides)

Estate	Demesne hides	Tenant hides	Ratio
Altwigshagen	7	14.5	1 : 2
Bilow	6	12	1 : 2
Broock	18.5	80	1 : 4.3
Damban	3	>6	c.1 : 2
Drake	10	46	1 : 4.6
Görmin (1574)	18.75	130.5	1 : 7
Görmin (1605)	45.25	104	1 : 2.3
Krackow	34	30.5	>1 : 1
Krackewitz	39.5	110.75	1 : 2.8
Passow	6	17	1 : 2.8
Pustow	12	22.25	1 : 1.9
Ribnitz	2354*	7040*	1 : 3
Ramin	56	186	1 : 3.3
Rothenklempenow	>8	62	c.1 : 7.75
Siedenbollentin	9.5	24	1 : 2.5
Wussow	32	133.75	1 : 4.2
Sum**	294.5	911.25	1 : 3.1

Notes: *In *scheffel* seed.
      ** Without Ribnitz.
Source: [102, 145].

lords to increase tenant cash rents. Thus, noble lords in particular shifted to demesne farming based on an increase of labour rents. Despite these changes, demesne land accounted only for 15 per cent of the area of noble and bourgeois estates and less than that of royal ones by c.1700 (the overall average was about 8 to 10 per cent). In 1770, 30 per cent of noble estates were without demesne farms, but 75 per cent of church and royal ones [14, 88].

Although demesne farms were established in central and southern Sweden, the total area was very small in Sweden and Finland, amounting to about 6 to 7 per cent of total land. Only in the province of Scania did two phases of demesne expansion in the sixteenth and late eighteenth centuries lead to a higher share of demesne land of about 10 per cent in 1658, rising to 25 per cent by 1800 [91].

East Prussian data (Table 4.3) also reflect variation in the proportion of demesne land between different types of estates. Overall,

Table 4.3 Demesne and tenant land in East
Prussia, c.1800 (%)

	Demesne	**Tenant**
Royal estates	7.0	93.0
Noble estates	61.6	38.4

Source: [60].

subject and free tenant farmers held nearly two-thirds of the
agricultural land in 1800. These data obscure the fact that there
was also considerable short-term fluctuation in demesne areas
following trends in grain prices. On East Prussian princely estates,
demesne arable farming areas reached their peak in the 1570s,
were then considerably reduced until the 1590s, rose again and
then decreased dramatically after 1610 [183]. Similar dynamics
could be expected in many estates throughout East-Central and
Eastern Europe (see above for Schleswig-Holstein) and can only be
determined by detailed case studies.

In sixteenth-century Livonia and Estonia, demesne grain
farming also expanded. Further growth was far from being a
continuous process, as many demesne farms had been destroyed
or abandoned during the Polish-Swedish War (1600–29) and the
Northern War (1655–60). After a new wave of expansion and a
simultaneous resettlement of tenants [34, 95, 100], development was
again severely interrupted by the Great Northern War (1700–21).
Demesne fields accounted for 23 to 27 per cent of the land in late
seventeenth-century Estonia (Table 4.4a).

During the second half of the eighteenth century, demesne farming in Russia began to expand in the more fertile and newly colonised
black-earth (*chernozem*) zones due to the growing integration of the
domestic market. This continued in some areas until the first half
of the nineteenth century. The period that saw the full expansion of
demesne farming thus seems rather brief compared to other territories
[216]. The literature assumes a regional economic division between
chernozem regions and others less suitable for agriculture, but this view
seems to underestimate regional variation in both areas [216, 221]
(Table 4.5). The relatively high land-to-labour ratio in Russia meant
that demesne growth was checked by the scarcity of labour.

Table 4.4 Relationship between demesne and tenant land in Eastern Baltic countries

Period	Ratio demesne/ tenant land	Note
(a) Estonia, 1550–c.1840		
1550	1 : 4.5–1 : 9	–
c.1600	1 : 4	Tartu Bishopric and southern Estonia
1690–1700	1 : 2.8	northern Estonia
c.1800	1 : 1.6–2.6	estimate noble estates
c.1840	1 : 2.8	estimate crown estates
(b) Livonia, 1600–1800		
1500–50	1 : 4	–
1600	1 : 3	–
1688	1 : 3.2	–
c.1800	1 : 1.5	140 estates in the Duchy of Courland

Source: [93, 96, 98, 101].

Table 4.5 Proportion of demesne land, Russia 1765–1858 (%)

Region	Proportion of demesne land	
	1765	**1858**
Central non-*chernozem*	26–28	45.3
Central *chernozem*	26–36	54.7

Source: [221].

After some initial growth before 1540, the main expansion of demesne farming in the Electorate of Brandenburg occurred between 1540–80 and 1620. Recent research illustrating the degree to which initial demesne building depended on villagers' cooperation rates the Brandenburg development 'as symbiotic with, rather than destructive of, the villagers' [116]. This may apply to many other areas of East-Central and Eastern Europe as well. Between 1470 and 1624, demesne land in the Brandenburg Middle Mark more than doubled from 1265 to 3164 hides [123]. By 1800, the number of demesne hides had reached 4820 [22, 115]. As in other territories affected by the Thirty Years' War, further extension immediately after 1648 was limited. In this period, new demesnes were built primarily by absorbing land deserted by tenants during the conflict [17]. A new expansion and intensification of the demesne economy had set in by the early eighteenth century. Increasing resistance by villagers supported by state court rulings often managed to hold the resulting burdens in check [118, 123]. More extreme proportions of demesne land – close to and above 40 per cent of the total – remained limited to a mere two of the twelve administrative districts of the Electorate west of the river Oder (Table 4.6).

Table 4.6 Proportion of demesne land in the Brandenburg Kurmark, 1797 (% of total winter seed)

District	Proportion of demesne land
Luckenwalde	16.1
Zauche	24.6
Niederbarnim	25.5
Beeskow	26.1
Teltow	27.0
Prignitz	27.7
Oberbarnim	28.4
Ruppin	31.6
Lebus	33.3
Havelland	34.8
Glien	37.3
Uckermark	43.8
Kurmark (total average)	33.3

Source: [16].

In Hungary, demesne farming expanded from the 1530s and 1540s; after 1550, the Slovakian part of the kingdom followed. The development was largely limited to regions with privileged access to grain markets and lasted until the first half of the seventeenth century. Further extension on deserted tenant land occurred in some regions after 1650, but in others abandoned demesnes were leased to tenants. In this period demesne growth was concentrated in the Habsburg regions. As in the eastern Baltic, wars prevented

Table 4.7 Proportion of demesne and tenant land in Hungary, 1580–1790 (%)

Period	Demesne	Tenant
1580	16.7	83.3
c.1600	15–30	70–85
1650	5–30	–
c.1790	27	–

Note: 1580, Four counties only.
Source: [55, 155].

continuous development, although previously held opinions that demesne activities were completely suspended for some time after 1650 were refuted by research after 1945.

Although many estates, especially in the west and north of Hungary, may have continued demesne activities throughout the seventeenth century, further major expansion probably only occurred after the 1730s and 1740s [155, 159]. Like in Poland, commercial demesnes were not usual on the property of the numerous smaller gentry.

Despite a visible tendency towards an intensification of subjection during the sixteenth century, the demesne economy remained relatively limited in parts of Silesia, though it would be wrong to underestimate its significance. In the lowland zones demesne farming was widespread, but it was not totally absent in mountainous regions either. A relatively stronger trend towards demesne building has been noted for Upper Silesia, the eastern part of the Duchy, where the share of demesne land probably grew to a third of the total [162, 171, 196]. Similar regional differences prevailed in Upper Lusatia. A dense demesne economy was characteristic of noble estates in certain areas. There were about 220 to 230 demesne farms in total in 1620, rising to 410 by 1800 [103].

There has been some debate as to whether the Thirty Years' War formed a qualitative break in the development of the demesne economy in Bohemia and Moravia (see Chapter 3, Section iv). Nevertheless, initial tendencies to establish demesne enterprises occurred from the late fifteenth century onwards and intensified during the sixteenth century, just as elsewhere. The growth of demesne arable farming was preceded in some regions by

Table 4.8 Proportion of demesne (arable) land in Bohemia and Moravia, 1600 to 1785–9 (%)

Period	Proportion of demesne land	
	Bohemia	**Moravia**
c.1600	20	–
c.1700	20–25	–
1720–50	24.3*	16
1785–9	24	12.8

Note: *Including demesne land leased to tenants.
Source: [1, 20].

investments in fish farming and intensified with the growing interest in demesne brewing after 1530–50 [42, 66, 76, 79, 80, 86]. On average, shares of demesne arable land (Table 4.8) did not reach high levels in Bohemia and Moravia. In individual regions more suitable for arable agriculture, such as the districts of Klatovsko or Kouřimsko in Central Bohemia, demesne farming developed more intensively. There, proportions of demesne land reached 40 per cent in the first half of the eighteenth century. Bohemia and Moravia were classic examples of a growing diversification of demesne economic activities (see Section v).

In some territories and regions, but not, for instance, in Russia and the Baltic, noble lords and particularly princely estates shifted towards abandoning direct management by dissolving or leasing demesne farms during the eighteenth century. This was partly a reaction to swings in agricultural prices such as in Schleswig-Holstein beginning in the 1730s, when quite a number of demesne farms were dissolved and tenants, who were allowed to purchase their farms in hereditary tenure, received freedom from bondage [134]. Trends following swings in agrarian business cycles were not unknown in earlier periods either. Economic pressure, for instance, prompted the duke and some of the nobles to lease out their demesne farms in Western Pomerania after 1600, often to the burghers of nearby towns [145] (for leases in seventeenth-century Estonia see [100]). According to the 1703 tax survey, as many as half of the demesne farms on princely estates and about 16 per cent on noble estates in Mecklenburg-Schwerin were leased [143]. Leaseholders could be nobles, burghers but also villagers. In the Mecklenburg village of Schönbeck, the princely estate administration leased the local demesne farm to the village headman and six serf farmers in 1726. This 'collective' worked the farm at least until 1787 and even extended the area leased in the 1750s [128]. In Western Pomerania, all princely estates were leased after 1766–70. In the 1780s, entire villages and their demesnes were leased to their inhabitants. This required considerable investment in the initial payment, but rents were relatively low and, above all, labour rents had ended. In eighteenth-century Brandenburg too, demesne farms were frequently leased to townsmen or tenant farmers (individually or collectively), usually to the highest bidder. Farms were also partitioned among villagers [106]. In Zealand, three-quarters of the demesne farms were worked under short-term leases after 1760 [88].

The early modern demesne economy was neither uniform nor static across time and space, but instead dynamically adapted its size, organisation of work and agricultural techniques according to business cycles and changing views on management practices. The survey has confirmed that despite the widespread start of demesne activities during the sixteenth century, this was not necessarily a continuous process. Consequently, the share of demesne land varied strongly. It represented a relatively large proportion in eastern Holstein, Mecklenburg and Pomerania (with an estimated 40 to 50 per cent of the land) and remained rather limited (with an estimated 20 to 30 per cent) for instance in the western and southern parts of the Electorate of Brandenburg or in Bohemia. Like Brandenburg, Silesia and Upper Lusatia were also regionally divided as to the importance of demesne farming. This, however, was typical even for countries associated with stricter forms of demesne lordship, such as Mecklenburg or Schleswig-Holstein [17, 134]. The landlords' share was usually larger with respect to pastures and particularly forests than to arable land.

[iv]   Labour Rents

The commercial demesne economy was not operated only with labour rents (*corvée*). Usually it relied on a mixture of (mostly unpaid) labour rents, wage labour and forced wage labour [34], the balance among which was subject to enormous variation between regions and periods. The usual explanation for the use of labour rents refers to the relatively low population density in Eastern Europe, which caused a high land-to-labour ratio (a shortage of labour and an abundance of land). This approach seems too simplistic. For instance, it does not explain why demesne lords took the same measures in territories with a comparatively high population density, even by Western standards, such as in Upper Lusatia, Lower Silesia, Bohemia, Moravia or parts of Little Poland, let alone the consideration that there usually were significant differences in population density between regions of all the other territories as well.

Research usually regards the obligation to render labour rents for the demesne economy as the most important economic characteristic of (hereditary) subjection and serfdom. According to the conventional interpretation, labour rents contributed profoundly to profitability of the demesnes. Tenant households supplied *corvée* as part of their rent obligations. Obligations included regular work on demesne farms (such as ploughing, manuring, harvesting, threshing or maintenance work) and sometimes less regular, yet more burdensome, work in the carting and haulage of goods (for instance timber, grain, beer or wine), repair work, building and a range of 'extraordinary' (that is, not included in the usual services) duties such as work in forestry or to provide firewood. The importance of each of these activities relative to the total workload of labour rents varied with the seasons. Fieldwork was concentrated in spring, summer and early autumn, haulage during harvest and the winter months [100, 123]. Villagers were also called to work in noble textile manufactories or iron mills, for instance in Bohemia, Moravia, the Polish Commonwealth, Upper Silesia and Russia [68, 72, 212].

A great deal of information exists about the levels of *corvée* that could theoretically be demanded by estate registers and terriers. The maximum was often regulated by law or local custom, but only case studies can determine the actual burdens, which could fluctuate from year to year. Depending on several factors, the extent of labour rents varied strongly. In many regions they did not exist at all or households paid cash in lieu, because lords did not need them. The level depended, among other factors, on the actual nature of demesne activities, the number of available villagers and the proportion of demesne land, and not least on policy shifts in estate management regarding whether or not to use *corvée* at all.

Full farms usually sent ploughing teams, whereas smallholders or cottagers provided manual labour. Before the sixteenth century, many cottagers and lodgers (see Chapter 5, Section iv) may have been exempt from *corvée*, unless they had been specifically settled as demesne workers during the Late Middle Ages [69]. There is an important distinction between practices in which obligations were more or less clearly specified, usually a maximum number of days per week (*gemessen*), and others in which they were theoretically unlimited (*ungemessen*) or, as for the late Middle Ages, not specified in detail, so subject to periodic renegotiation. With good reason, the literature concludes that labour rents (and other burdens) could not be raised too far without threatening the viability of the tenant economy and it is clear that lords were aware of being dependent on villagers' work [3, 112].

Sixteenth- and seventeenth-century laws enabled demesne lords to force villagers' children to enter agricultural service on demesne farms (*Gesindezwang*). The term during which these girls and boys were paid wages as servants was usually limited to three to five years [22, 42, 80, 103, 123, 183, 193]. For instance in Brandenburg, this practice was first established in 1518 and confirmed in various new ordinances during the sixteenth and seventeenth centuries [22, 123]. In Western Pomerania, it was usual from the beginning of the sixteenth century. In Upper Lusatia, forced service with prescribed wages was first implemented in 1539 and regulations were repeated and extended in land ordinances until 1767 [103]. Resolutions of the Silesian Diet that set out ordinances for servants and obligatory service were passed in 1502, 1512, 1528 and 1565 and standardised in the 1652 Ordinance for Servants and Subjects. In Mecklenburg, forced service was usual, but does not seem to have been formally introduced by law [22]. As with seignorial jurisdiction, forced service was also far from universal in East-Central and Eastern Europe. In Poland, Slovakia, Hungary and even Mecklenburg, for instance, such regulations did not exist.

Lords used a variety of methods to raise labour rents beyond the usual medieval levels of a few days per year when their demand for labour increased due to the growth of demesne farming. First, new obligations were frequently established by negotiations with villagers, with seignorial pressure and force growing over time. Tenant farmers and smallholders may initially have consented to occasional and very limited labour services. Often requested rather than commanded, they were sometimes introduced by means of formal contracts between lords and villagers in exchange for reducing payments, dues or additional tenant land. For instance, lords offered more land to cottagers and asked for higher weekly labour services in return [106, 113, 115]. Some time in the fifteenth and early sixteenth centuries, when inflation had eroded much of the original value of their cash rents, the rural population may have consented to rendering *corvée*, especially when levels were still low. Demesne lords may have needed labour desperately, due to the lack of servants or wage labourers and high wage levels.

Contracts between Brandenburg lords and their tenants occasionally stipulated that both sides were allowed to choose between paying rent and performing labour. In the estate of Stavenow, farmers only agreed to provide more labour rents when their rents in cash and especially those in kind were held constant or reduced, and they also went to court to secure their demands. During the sixteenth century, reduced rents in kind meant that a higher proportion of grain could be marketed and would provide a rising income for villagers despite their rendering *corvée* [113, 119, 148]. But if grain prices were low, a shift from cash rents to services brought other advantages for villagers. In depressed markets they faced difficulties in selling the necessary quantities of grain to raise the money for rents. As a consequence, villagers moved away from estates where cash rents were demanded to those where they could render labour rents instead. A Polish regulation of 1520, which set a maximum for labour rents, has been argued not to be a measure to protect villagers' rights but a means to prevent the general undermining of cash rents and to protect the properties of the gentry, who were dependent on cash rents rather than on the extraction of labour [163]. Medieval conversions into cash rents generally remained in place in villages that were too far from any place where their labour may have been needed [106]. In addition, if villagers were unwilling to negotiate, no bargain offered by the lord would help. In 1612, villagers on the Brandenburg estate of Wilsnack were promised food and drink if they would help in harvesting oat and barley, but they declined all the same [135]. Labour rents first increased at a time of growing income for tenant farmers during the sixteenth century, so maybe they were able to absorb some of the pressure without any significant loss of income.

The development of labour rents is best described as a process of negotiation that took several steps before demesne lords could impose labour rents on their own, probably with the help of state authorities and law. Negotiations often led to the conclusion of formal contracts [106, 113]. These were frequently accompanied by conflicts and demesne lords exerted various degrees of pressure, including outright violence or imprisonment of those who resisted their claims. The lord of Stavenow estate only renewed the grazing rights of villagers in 1543 when they accepted new labour rents on top of the payments they already rendered [113]. Some households of a village sometimes already performed labour rents and lords used this fact to extend them to the others [106, 119]. Nevertheless, villagers were aware of possible weaknesses. Realising that their lord would lose his Uckermark estate because of indebtedness, they simply refused to render any labour rents while this power vacuum lasted in 1649–50 [106].

Due to sixteenth-century population growth, lords were in a better bargaining position than a century earlier when they needed to attract tenants (and normally had no use for their services in any case). Once these demands were negotiated and in place, it was difficult to remove them. Constant resistance against increasing demands by demesne lords, who tried to undermine earlier agreements, became the rule [106]. In 1639, officials in Mecklenburg continued to demand labour rents in spite of the duke's agreement to relieve his tenants on the island of Poel from their obligations in exchange for an annual payment of a certain quantity of barley. When they complained, the duke upheld the original burdens in violation of the new agreement [106, 112, 128]. Brandenburg tenants fought fierce legal battles with their lords over binding arrangements for labour rents from the 1540s on. In many cases they turned to the ruler to demand that a solution be decreed or existing contracts be obeyed. The villagers of Groß Möringen appear as a group of insubordinates who fought all their demesne lords between 1554 and 1607 because of each lord's desire to increase labour rents as soon as he had taken over the village from his predecessor. The situation was resolved in 1607 with a contract that specified how many days were demanded, what was to be done in case less happened to be required, what the daily working hours were, whether food and drink were to be provided and so on [106]. Sometimes, outright injustice prevailed. Certain events facilitated the introduction of or sudden increase in labour rents. A temporary absence of lordship could accompany a generational change in estate owners [123, 135], but a change in estate ownership might enable a new lord to extend labour rents, if villagers lacked written proof of previous custom. There was also the notorious case when nobles controlled pawned estates in exchange for credit (usually given to the territorial prince) for a limited period. The creditor then received the estate's income instead of interest payments, which led to pressure to maximise the proceeds by means of raising the burdens. Often these properties were transferred to the creditors in the end, because the ruler could not pay back the loan, so the exceptional burdens ended up being regular ones.

Polish villagers are usually regarded as having been confronted rather early with increases in labour rents. In 1421, a regulation by Mazovian noblemen set the usual burden of labour rents at one day per week (repeated for Red Ruthenia in 1477). It is estimated that about a third of the farms in Mazovia actually performed these and it seems that commutation into money was comparatively expensive. A workload of one day per week for a fullholding is widely regarded as usual for fifteenth-century Poland and it is repeated in several contemporary regulations, among them the famous Statute of Toruń of 1520. According to a survey for 300 of the Archbishop of Gniezno's villages in 1511 and 136 of the Bishop of Włocławek's in 1534, 20 to 30 per cent of the villages performed labour services of two to three days a week. For most this increased to three days until 1582 [55, 115, 163, 197]. For the second half of the sixteenth century, two days and more had become usual in several parts of the kingdom, while in 1500–50 the average had been 1.7 days (Table 4.9).

Demands may have reached a threshold of three days a week around 1600. In the Sandomierz district, two days of draught services and four days of manual services were usual for a full tenant farm in the second half of the sixteenth century. After 1600, this doubled to two days' draught services from a half holding and four days' from a full farm [160, 170, 174, 189, 194, 197, 203]. In the district of Korczyn, the average number of work days per household increased from 1.87 per week in 1572 to 2.5 in 1616–29 and 2.54 in 1660. Extreme demands for labour services of four or five days a week may have occurred in the first half of the seventeenth century in parts of Great Poland [28, 181, 199]. These increases may have been due to widespread desertions, which meant that the necessary services were left to the remaining tenants.

Table 4.9 Labour rent demands on noble estates in Poland, 1551–80 (number of villages and their labour service obligations in days per week)

Region	2 days	3 days	4 days	Average no. of days/week
Western Great Poland	2	10	7	3.26
Eastern Great Poland	2	–	1	2.67
Mazovia	3	–	1	2.5
Little Poland	1	6	–	2.86
Total	8	16	9	3.03

Source: [197].

Labour rents in eighteenth-century Poland could be high in comparison to other areas. However, tenants were compensated by the fact that other dues and even taxes were relatively low. Levels alternated between one and six days a week, but there were also regions and social groups that were not affected. Primarily cash rents were charged, for instance in Royal Prussia and areas of Great Poland. More than 40 per cent of royal villages in the mountainous regions of the Cracow area did not owe labour rents in the late eighteenth century. By around 1720, the rural population of Lithuanian royal estates provided mainly cash rents [115, 161, 165, 170, 185, 191, 202].

For the Kingdom of Bohemia, scholarly opinion has always been divided as to whether the systematic use of labour rents had begun before 1620–50 (see Chapter 3, Section iv). Although a gradual extension during the sixteenth century has frequently been acknowledged [5, 80], recent case studies on several large noble estate complexes found evidence of a systematic use of wage labour for the expanding demesne economy in this period and a wider shift to labour rents only after 1650 [1, 20, 66, 67, 76, 80]. For sixteenth-century Moravia, studies assume a combination of wage work and labour rents. A more systematic use of labour rents during the later seventeenth and eighteenth centuries is uncontested, but average burdens never reached the values of the more extreme zones of demesne lordship. There were many estates with a lower intensity of demesne farming, especially after 1700 [1, 20, 79]. State regulations stipulated a maximum of three days of labour rents per week from 1680. These were repated at various points during the eighteenth century following resistance and uprisings against labour rents and taxes [1, 69, 80]. A mix between estates with higher labour rents and regions with very little demesne farming activities was also characteristic for the neighbouring territories of Upper Lusatia and Lower Silesia [103, 171].

On Mecklenburg noble estates, labour rents may have increased from one to two days per week before 1550 to two to three days per full tenant farm towards the end of the century. In 1595, a document refers for the first time to the fact that services of three days per week were usual. In princely estates the development was slower, but by 1650 service levels had also reached three to four days a week [128, 129]. It is not entirely clear whether Mecklenburg lords were able to increase labour rents further after the Thirty Years' War without risking villagers escaping (see Chapter 3, Section iv). Despite their weak legal position, villagers did not simply obey the rising burdens. When the princely estate of Schwerin added another day of forced labour per week in 1655, farmers stated that it was impossible for them. Their threat to run away helped and the administration relented [128].

Indirect evidence from a 1703 tax survey in Mecklenburg-Schwerin points to significant differences between princely and noble estates in this respect. Princely demesne farms had on average two to three times as many tenant households to provide labour services. Tenant farmers on noble estates kept on average about 10 per cent more horses and cattle, presumably because of the higher burden of labour rents per holding [143]. An increase in labour demand resulted from the introduction of *Schlagwirtschaft* (see Chapter 5, Section ii), which was met by a growing importance for the wage labour of smallholders and cottagers after 1750. There was fierce competition for wage labour, which was also needed in tenant households. In the 1790s, services were abolished on the princely estates [127].

For Western Pomerania, the literature concludes that labour rents of two to three days per week were usual at the beginning of the seventeenth century. Yet there remained a number of areas where villagers were not drafted to perform services and paid cash rents in lieu. Many of the smaller estates probably did not have enough tenant farms to work their demesne farms with services only [145].

After 1650, it seems that services were increased beyond three days a week. By the late seventeenth century, nearly two-thirds (65.8 per cent) of the tenant farms and smallholdings in Western Pomerania had to render services [144]. On princely estates in Western Pomerania, labour rents with four horses could be demanded from a full tenant farmer on six days a week at the end of the seventeenth and the first half of the eighteenth century. Table 4.10 lists duties recorded in a cadastral survey.

Of the more than 3300 tenant holdings recorded in total, a significant minority of 17.8 per cent rendered cash rents only. On church estates, less than half the holdings (49.4 per cent) were obliged to provide labour rents. In the princely estate of Eldena, 60.4 per cent of the holdings only paid cash rents [144].

In eastern Schleswig-Holstein, the establishment of daily services occurred during the sixteenth century. In extreme cases, burdens for fullholdings further increased to up to two teams of draught animals on five to six days per week [134, 148]. For demesne dairy farming, which was widespread, waged servants were hired. On some princely estates, the necessary investments for an extension of demesne farming were not made and instead income was increased by converting excess labour rents into payments in lieu from the 1590s onwards. This policy was systematically extended on princely estates after 1630 [139].

Table 4.10 Labour rents in Western Pomerania according to the 1692–8 cadastral survey (number of holdings and %)

	Full and half farmholdings		Smallholders	
Days/ week	Draught animals	Manual	Draught animals	Manual
0	68 (5.2)	459 (35.2)	488 (81.5)	51 (8.5)
1	11 (0.8)	583 (44.8)	0	35 (5.9)
2	80 (6.2)	160 (12.3)	14 (2.3)	41 (6.8)
3	477 (36.6)	48 (3.7)	53 (8.8)	196 (32.7)
4	330 (25.3)	21 (1.6)	13 (2.2)	131 (21.9)
5	65 (5.0)	3 (0.2)	3 (0.5)	49 (8.2)
6	272 (20.9)	29 (2.2)	28 (4.7)	96 (16.0)
Total	1303 (100.0)	1303 (100.0)	599 (100.0)	599 (100.0)

Source: [144].

An estimate suggests that at the height of this development, an average fullholder had to tend about 60 hectares of demesne farmland on top of his own holding that comprised about 50 hectares (and was thus substantially larger than the average fullholding in Eastern Europe). Around 1770, fullholdings sent four horses and three workers (usually a male servant, a maid servant and a young man) to work on the demesnes. Landless households sent a worker on two to three days a week for manual labour. However, both groups had to pay only minimal rents in cash or in kind and state taxes were paid by the demesne lord [148]. Seignorial attempts to raise services did not remain unchecked, nevertheless. Serfs resisted if they felt that custom was violated and their petitions were supported by state authorities, such as in the case of the estate of Seedorf in 1723, when the lord was told to maintain labour rents at the level he had promised when he took over the estate. In Holstein princely estates, the demesne economy operated predominantly with wage labourers, supported by the manual labour rents of cottagers [112, 139, 140].

In Denmark, about 40 per cent of all tenant farms on noble estates were liable to render labour rents and 17 per cent on royal ones after 1650. In 1770, 85 per cent of the tenants of Zealand, 73 per cent on Funen and 72 per cent in Jutland owed labour rents. On individual estates, lords demanded considerable labour services in the eighteenth century, but overall the burden remained milder than in the districts of demesne lordship in neighbouring Schleswig-Holstein. In case studies, an annual burden for fullholders of up to 300 days has been found for the late 1700s. Each farmer had to tend approximately 2.2 to 2.8 hectares of demesne land. In the village of Giesegaard (Zealand), the 210 days demanded in 1780 were divided into 12 days of ploughing with six horses and two servants, 46 days with two horses and 152 days on which one worker or one boy or girl had to be sent [14, 88].

In the Swedish province of Scania, the average number of *corvée* days per tenant per year grew from 83 in 1750 to 314 in 1850. In the rest of Sweden, *corvée* was regulated by law and by the limited number of demesnes [90, 91]. Labour rents also existed in Finland, but the density of demesne farming remained low. As in most parts of Sweden, villages close to demesne farms were particularly affected and weekly burdens could reach two to three days, while many other villages paid in lieu of services [14].

Several authors documented intensive conflicts in Brandenburg over rising labour rents after the fifteenth century [106, 118]. During the sixteenth century, systematic pressure to extend labour rents increased. Resistance, such as by three tenants in Lützlow in 1554, drew retaliation by lords; in this case he banned them from water supplies and from the use of pastures. Two days of labour per week were defined as customary in 1572 and two to three days became widespread until 1620. In certain regions, such as in the Lebus area, extreme burdens of up to five days occurred. On the estate of Stavenow, regulations established in 1549 demanded that fullholders send a ploughing team for three days a week and cottagers owed three days of manual labour each week [106, 113, 119, 123].

When at the end of the seventeenth century demesne lords began to demand daily and unrestricted services, villagers refused to render them for lengthy periods. The re-introduction of labour services on the Neumark estates of the Knights of the Order of St John in 1770 met with resistance from the rural population and only some of them were established in an agreement between the Order and the villagers, reached after lengthy protests and negotiations [123]. Everywhere, the prescribed levels could differ from those delivered. The tenant farmers of Badingen reported that they rendered up to four days weekly, although official registers listed up to six [106, 116]. On the estate of Boitzenburg, the total annual burden was calculated as 78 days with a team of draught animals and 48 days of manual labour of one person, including carting services [118]. If tenants were only leaseholders, they could frequently reduce the level of labour rents and partly commute them to cash payments when leases were renewed in the period after 1700 [106].

In two princely estates in East Prussia, services increased from one day a week to two or three days between 1550 and 1609–10 due to the expansion of demesne land. As the number of tenants had not grown to the same degree on sixteenth-century noble estates, burdens were probably higher than on princely ones. With population growth and stagnant agricultural prices, demesne expansion halted on princely estates and services that were no longer needed were abolished and converted into cash rents around 1600 [183]. In the long run, this led to two groups in the subject population: one rendering labour rents (*Scharwerker*) and the other paying increased cash rents in lieu of services (*Hochzinser*) [60]. When population levels fell, the burdens of the remaining tenants could increase. Ten princely demesnes could use the labour rents of 1355 tenant farmers in 1610; in 1683, only 530 farmers were still available. With the extension of their land, these demesne farms reduced the number of continuously employed servants over the course of the seventeenth century from 409 to 285. In 1664, tenant farmers of Bal'ga complained that they had to send one servant and one maid to work on the demesne farm every day during the summer season, as well as another servant sent with a plough team. They could not bear such burdens any longer (*'könnten so schwer scharwerk nicht mehr außstehen'*) [22, 183, 193].

In total, around 85 per cent of the tenant farmers on royal and nobles estates were liable to perform labour services in 1701. In some regions the proportion of farmers without labour rents could reach 30 per cent. By the late eighteenth century, 40 per cent of the population in royal estates performed labour rents [60]. On noble estates, the lower number of tenants determined that they had to put up with labour rents of up to 250 days per year, in more extreme cases even between 251 and 500, which would mean that farms kept one or two labourers only for work on the demesnes. In three districts, the share of tenants who had to supply the highest number of labour services varied between 5 and 77 per cent during the eighteenth century. In regions remote from markets, villagers may have preferred this regulation over one in which labour rents were abolished in exchange for high cash rents [60].

In Hungary, a 1514 law established that each farm had to supply labour rents of one day per week. This formed an important basis for lords to extend services, but it did not necessarily mean that they became universal. In the third quarter of the sixteenth century, labour rents could reach two or, especially during the summer season, three days a week, particularly in areas with good marketing conditions. Particularly until the 1570s, wage labour was used more frequently to run the demesnes and sometimes villagers received compensation even for labour services. Viticulture was usually based on wage labour [14, 55, 155, 159]. In some Ottoman areas villagers were occasionally called for labour rents. The generally greater involvement of demesne lords in trade with wine and sometimes grain meant that tenants were usually less burdened with work on demesnes, but that lords required them to haul the goods to markets over great distances.

In the principalities of Wallachia and Moldavia (Ottoman Empire), labour rents were limited to a small number of days per year and any increase was highly contested, because state regulations established maximum burdens. Market incentives for expansion of the demesne economy remained limited until the late eighteenth century. With the exception of Hungarian western Wallachia, where labour rents increased to a maximum of one day per week, the demesne economies of Moldavia and Wallachia concentrated first on animal husbandry, where practically no labour rents were used [157].

In Estonia and Livonia, increases in labour rents occurred after 1550, when a regular number of work days per week were established during the peak summer season. Demesne farming was probably not fully developed by 1600. In only 4 of a sample of 25 estates were more than half the rural households liable for labour rents. However, where labour rents were recorded, they could be high – up to five days a week with one or two workers for a fullholding [95, 98]. Labour services became more dominant in the seventeenth century when protests against the burdens are recorded. Whether a 1687 Swedish royal decree or the state land revision (cadastre) of 1696 brought improvements is contested, partly because services were frozen at the high levels they had already reached before. In the late 1600s it seemed widespread to demand one man with a team of draught animals year round and additional days of manual labour during the summer. Russian authorities (from 1721) accepted Swedish regulations and they were supervised on the basis of new land revisions [94, 97, 98]. An analysis of more than 3000 Estonian farms shows that about two-thirds had to provide a plough team on one or two days and less than 30 per cent three days per week. Only about 6 per cent of the farms had to render services four days a week [96, 98].

The eighteenth-century expansion in demesnes, especially in the *chernozem* zones, caused a strong overall shift towards labour rents instead of quitrents in Russia. Three days of services a week were regarded as usual. The specific problem was the concentration in an extremely short agricultural season [214, 215]. The increase of labour rents over the eighteenth century represented a significantly greater additional burden for tenant households than the simultaneous increase of quitrent [222]. The organisation of work and the level of control are reflected in case studies. Large tenant households cultivated more than 20 acres of their own land, approximately 13.5 acres of demesne arables and up to 3.5 acres of demesne hayfield in the early nineteenth century [214]. According to a survey in seven of the *chernozem* provinces in the late eighteenth century, between 36 and 92 per cent of the tenant households rendered labour rents. *Barshchina* dominated in 5 of these provinces. By contrast, *obrok* dominated in 8 of 13 non-*chernozem* provinces (the range was between 21 and 85 per cent of rural households). The highest percentage of villagers with *barshchina* obligations occurred in Pskov (79 per cent) and in Tula and Kursk (92 per cent) [209, 221, 225]. Just before the 1861 reforms, over half of the demesne lords in central *chernozem* estates reported that they required three days a week, around a quarter as high as four days. In total, only about slightly more than a fifth of all rural households (or 55 per cent of the farms on noble estates) rendered labour, many at a very low level and mixed with cash rents, while the rest of the noble subjects and all villagers on state estates paid quitrent [221].

High labour rents of three days or more a week were very rare outside the area of demesne lordship. They are regarded as the major factor that negatively influenced the economy of tenant households, as they drew manpower and draught animals to the demesne sector. For burdens higher than two or three days a week, households were most likely forced to keep an additional plough team for demesne work. These levels are usually regarded as the threshold of extreme forms of demesne lordship. However, rather than stereotypically repeating that labour rents could represent a significant burden, as the literature does, we should turn to the far more interesting question of how tenant farms and smallholders coped with the economic challenges these imposed. The fact that they could cope and did so by various means should not surprise us. To begin with, decision making in this respect was largely left to villagers and their families. A preferred way was to send a servant or a day labourer to work for the lord. When villagers had a strong bargaining position, such as in Brandenburg after the Thirty Years' War, they tried to take advantage of the situation to opt out of labour rents altogether. Some paid considerable amounts of money in order to do so [34, 108, 115, 148]. The actual performance of labour rents was spread unevenly within and between villages. There were important differences between the number of work days demanded in regulations and those actually performed. Although the number performed could be higher than documents stipulated (this will have been the case especially in the initial phases of rising labour rents), the prescribed number of days usually exceeded the needs of the demesne economy. For instance, in the Holstein estate of Schönweide, only 9379 work days (69.4 per cent) out of a norm of 13 524 were performed in 1798 [138]. In the Northern Bohemian estates Frýdlant and Liberec, between 25 and 30 per cent of rural households completely avoided their labour rents by cash payments (and many more at least in part) [72]. Almost everywhere in regions with labour rents, substantial parts of the population did not render services because of special privileges or because they paid money in lieu.

As far as the organisation of work on demesnes is concerned, a mixed system, using labour rents as well as wage labour, prevailed in most regions [10]. Wage labour was always necessary on demesne farms for animal husbandry or for intensive cultivation like viticulture. As early as the sixteenth century, Mecklenburg and Schleswig-Holstein demesne farms regularly kept huge herds – up to 200 cattle, 1500 sheep and 200 pigs on larger farms. Intensive sheep breeding was also usual in Upper Lusatia, Silesia and the Czech Lands [67, 138, 140]. That number of cattle, as an example, would have needed the continuous care of about 20 full-time maidservants, according to contemporary literature on good housekeeping.

Between 50 and 80 per cent (average 63 per cent) of the demesne area on Polish noble estates was cultivated with labour rents in the third quarter of the sixteenth century [160, 172, 197]. Data on several hundred royal, church and noble demesnes in three voivodships in Little Poland confirm that the vast majority – more than 80 per cent – also employed servants and seasonal wage labourers in the period 1525–1642. Demesnes based entirely on labour services formed the minority in Poland and did not occur at all in certain regions. Many gentry estates did not have enough tenants for their demesnes to be worked with labour rents [160, 173, 206]. In 1564, 40 per cent of the villages on royal estates in the Cracow region incurred duties only in cash and kind. By the second half of the eighteenth century this proportion had declined to 6 per cent, but a further 49 per cent of all villages commuted a part of their *corvée* obligations. The great majority of tenant farms in the Chełmno voivodship did not render labour rents at this time [161, 165, 191]. There were considerable fluctuations between a greater share of labour rents and wage labour on East Prussian princely demesnes around 1600. Excess labour rents were converted into cash payments in lieu. The estate administration was flexible and aimed to generate more income with the additional rent when demand for grain was slack, for instance in 1590 and 1610, but also raised the income necessary to increase the number of waged servants on demesnes. On the estate of Ostróda, *corvée* was converted into payments in 1615 and then reintroduced in 1622. Other reasons were that some villages were too far away to perform regular services on certain farms, or that demesnes had been leased and the labour rents were no longer needed [183].

From 657 demesne farms surveyed in Western Pomerania just before 1700, 421 (61.1 per cent) were operated with labour rents and 165 (25.1 per cent) were run entirely with servants and wage labour (for a further 71 farms there is no information). Small demesne farms in particular were more likely to be worked with servants [144]. The proportion of noble demesnes worked without labour rents was comparatively high, about 20 to 25 per cent around 1630, probably fuelled by the lack of tenants due to the Thirty Years' War [145]. Many of the demesne farms on smaller noble estates were relatively better equipped with their own draught animals, certainly compared to princely demesne farms in the country, simply because these properties did not have a sufficient number of tenant farmers to perform labour rents. In these cases, owners were forced to turn to wage labour or to different modes of operations such as leasing out demesnes.

In Mecklenburg a mixed system also prevailed, if only for lack of tenants (see above and Chapter 3, Section iv). In Brandenburg, some lords operated demesnes with their own draught animals and waged workers after the Thirty Years' War, again because of lack of tenants capable of providing labour rents [115]. In Boitzenburg, new demesne farms erected on deserted farmland between 1650 and 1700 were leased out to single tenants, who operated them with wage labour. When the estate returned to demesne farming after population and agrarian prices had consolidated, some of the farms continued to be run independently, while others were taken into direct management and re-introduced labour rents. After 1750, new demesne farms were either leased to bourgeois investors or tenant farmers or were managed directly with servants and wage labour [106, 118]. Thus, paradoxically, the extension of demesne farmland actually resulted in a shift towards wage labour supplied by cottagers and crofters. This also occurred in the last stage of

Mecklenburg demesne farming, before the abolition of serfdom in 1820. In Denmark, leaseholders of demesnes invested early in labour-saving techniques and machines. They were forced to cut labour costs, as they could not increase labour rents. Demesnes in direct seigneurial management also adopted such innovations when they led to higher profits, or when an attempted push for more labour rents faced the resistance of villagers or government restrictions [88].

In many regions of Eastern Europe there was a trend to convert labour rents into payments in lieu during the eighteenth century. These new receipts could represent up to 20 or 30 per cent of seignorial income [1, 34, 165]. Demesne farming increasingly turned to using a higher proportion of wage labour because of growing resistance against labour rents and the greater availability of workers due to population growth and social differentiation (see Chapter 5, Section iv). Often labour rents were abandoned or became a marginal phenomenon even before their legal abolition [115, 116]. On the Brandenburg estate of Boitzenburg, two-thirds of the demesne farms and three-quarters of the demesne land were operated with wage labour just before the agrarian reforms in 1800 [118].

The actual burden of labour rents varied considerably both chronologically and regionally. It was usual for not all tenant households to render labour rents. With the exception of Russia and Scania, the amount of labour rents theoretically available for the demesne economy possibly peaked during the eighteenth century due to population growth and seignorial pressures. On the other hand, demesne farming began to contract in some areas as early as the late seventeenth century. While tenants were still formally obliged to render labour rents, these increasingly were converted into cash payments in lieu. On the basis of this overall trend in the operation of demesnes and state-led measures to restrict the use of labour rents, some of the literature concludes that the eighteenth century witnessed structural changes and a loosening of seignorial relations in demesne lordship. The resistance of villagers played a major role in this process. Whether it is justified to interpret this as a trend towards the dissolution of demesne lordship even before the beginning of the great state-led reforms of relations between lords and villagers has been a matter of controversy.

[v]   Seignorial Monopolies, Breweries and Distilleries

Demesne lords were able to a certain extent to use their extra-economic powers to control markets and trade. Their power was mostly limited to an estate's internal market and would include certain monopolies: exclusive rights to supply alcoholic beverages, the existence of obligatory milling franchises for demesne mills and forced sales of products of the demesne economy (such as beer, spirits, cheese, wool, timber) to the local population. Another practice was to require villagers to offer their goods first to the lords, before releasing them for general sale. Comparable monopolies were not unknown in areas of the Central and Western European seignorial system either. In some countries lords challenged the trading and marketing privileges of towns and tried to establish control of the grain trade, which could harm the urban sector (see Chapter 3, Section iii) [123]. Trade privileges for nobles existed for example in Brandenburg, Hungary, Slovakia and Poland.

The building of closed estate markets seemed to have advanced particularly in sixteenth-century Bohemia, Moravia and Hungary [55, 80, 155]. One important element in the Czech Lands was the monopoly of beer produced in demesne breweries, while in Hungary the wine trade was of special significance. Seventeenth-century Hungarian estate accounts show that between half and two-thirds of annual cash income came from the sale of wine, supplemented sometimes by the sale of beer [1, 80, 155]. Yet, for instance in Hungary, independent selling of wine was never forbidden. Demesne breweries, distilleries and inns became a widespread and very profitable part of the demesne economy in many areas of East-Central and Eastern Europe. This could also have consequences for arable production on demesnes (for example a priority given to wheat and barley as the grains needed for brewing). In Bohemia, demesne breweries made up 43 per cent of gross seignorial income on average by the mid-eighteenth century [1, 67, 80]. In the Polish Commonwealth, the use of alcohol monopolies became very widespread during the eighteenth century. In royal estates, proceeds from the forced sale of spirits and beer (*propinacja*) increased from negligible amounts to 40 per cent of total income in 1789 [29, 55, 115, 182]. Estonian lords successfully exported spirits to Russia beginning in the 1760s, as well as achieving sales in taverns on their estates [93, 96, 98].

Villagers avoided monopolies or undermined their effectiveness by different means. For instance, in the Eastern Baltic in the seventeenth century, merchants of the port cities were in contact with tenant farmers and bought grain, cattle and other products directly, thus circumventing local seignorial market controls [101]. In Hungary, villagers' ability to market their products independently was not endangered [159]. Northern Bohemian villagers traded with princely towns in Upper Lusatia, but faced being punished by their demesne lord [68, 72]. As many fines issued for illegal taverns confirm, villagers persistently undermined seignorial monopolies [88]. Obstructing the independent marketing of tenant production was found impossible in Brandenburg [34, 106, 119, 120] and villagers were even able to profit from this market structure. Demesne breweries and distilleries, for instance, provided a continuous demand for grain from tenant agriculture. These purchases belonged to the largest expenses of the demesne economy [66].

Demesne agriculture also included dairy farming, the raising of sheep for the commercial sale of wool (demesne farms in Mecklenburg-Schwerin had between 300 and 400 sheep on average in 1702 [143]) and forestry. Most of the forests were landlord property and rents were collected from the villagers using them (for instance for herding their animals or burning charcoal). Demesne lords could derive some income from energy-intensive industries such as burning charcoal or potash, glass and iron making, bleaching or fulling mills. Timber was not only sold to villagers, which alone represented a significant profit, but also beyond estates. It was exported at a large scale from Poland, Prussia, Northern Bohemia and Moravia, Upper Silesia or the north-eastern Baltic. According to the accounts of the Duchy of Mecklenburg-Strelitz, the prince's income from forestry was almost as high as that from commercial demesne farms between 1704 and 1708 [128]. Selling timber was a continuous source of revenue, but it was also a way to increase income quickly without prior investments if necessary, because of debts or the complete failure of other enterprises (such as the destruction of demesne farms after a war) [116, 135].

[vi]   The Economic Fortunes of the Demesne Economy

The growing importance of the commercial demesne economy for seignorial income was one of the central economic characteristics of demesne lordship after the sixteenth century. Just like all the other elements, this pattern was not universal in East-Central and Eastern Europe. In fact, the structure of seignorial income changed significantly over time and important regional differences existed at all times. While one estate may have been characterised by a fully developed demesne economy, neighbouring ones in the same region partly or completely abandoned demesne activities (or never introduced them in the first place) and were more similar to the rent-based seignorial system found in Western and Southern ancien régime Europe.

For estates with a fully developed demesne economy, the overwhelming share of landlord income usually derived from this source. The proportion represented by cash or product rents declined and typically stagnated at between 10 and 33 per cent of total revenue. Regional variation did not follow the conditions of the natural environment as consistently as was previously thought. Studies for East Prussia and Estonia do not only provide good illustrations of important regional variations within the demesne economic structure, but also reflect significant medium-term patterns of change in the seignorial income structure. On two East Prussian princely estates, for example, income from the demesne economy fluctuated strongly during the sixteenth and early seventeenth centuries. On one estate demesne farming was the most important sector in the sixteenth century, but cash rents took the lead after 1600, while on the other cash rents were continually dominant [183]. On several Estonian and Livonian noble estates the demesne economy generated most of the income as early as 1550 [98], while royal estates were still based on rent, especially grain rents [93, 95]. The trend was towards a greater importance for demesne farming and the sale of beer during the later seventeenth century [94, 98, 100]. A general assessment shows that about half of estates were characterised by a developed demesne economy, whereas in the others villagers' rents remained the major source of income as late as the second half of the seventeenth century. Smaller estates in particular relied more heavily on demesnes, while larger ones leaned more towards tenant rents [94, 100]. In the early nineteenth century, between 60 and 100 per cent of the gross monetary income generated by the demesne economy came from the sale of spirits to traders or in local taverns [93].

Western Pomerania was a typical example of the significance of demesne farming. Grain sales represented only 27.5 per cent of overall income on princely estates in 1566–7 and more than doubled to 56.8 per cent in 1601–2. Between 50 per cent and 67 per cent of the rye and barley sold in 1566–7 and 1601–2 came from the harvests of the demesne farms, the rest from tenant product rents. By contrast, the value of tenant cash rents as a proportion of total income decreased from 31 to 7.2 per cent. Estimates of the income structure of noble estates based on estate valuations show that villagers' cash rents represented a third of income at most. Seignorial forestry or demesne farms were the most important sectors [145]. The income structure of estates in Mecklenburg in the early seventeenth century must have been similar. According to 73 valuations, demesne arable farming represented 68 per cent of the estate value and animal husbandry a further 18 per cent.

Cash and product rents remained roughly constant in the sixteenth-century Electorate of Brandenburg, but the major extension of demesne farming constituted a growing share of seignorial income. For instance, on six estates the demesne economy contributed between 30 and 80 per cent of annual seignorial income between 1553 and 1617 [118, 119]. Grain sales, but also timber, were the most important contributors to income at the Wilsnack estate [135]. On the estate of Stavenow in 1601, demesne production was estimated to represent nearly half the total value of the estate and labour rents 12.6 per cent, while the share of villagers' grain and cash rents was negligible [116]. According to annual accounts for 1746–59, nearly three-quarters of gross income (73.7 per cent) was derived from demesne arable and livestock farming. Villagers' rents in Boitzenburg in 1787–8 were only 18.1 per cent of the income from demesnes in direct management or in lease [118]. In eighteenth-century East Prussia, income from the noble demesne economy was estimated to represent 58 per cent of the total [60], but individual examples could display a far greater importance for cash rents.

In Denmark, seignorial income from the demesne economy could reach 70 to 80 per cent of the total on noble estates in which demesne farming was fully developed. However, 30 per cent of the noble estates and 75 per cent of royal and church ones were based entirely on the income of cash and product rents in 1770 [88]. The demesne economy dominated seignorial income on estates with demesnes in the Swedish province of Scania from the late seventeenth century onwards. Their share of income grew from 51 per cent to 81 per cent on average between 1675 and 1800 [91].

On Polish royal and noble estates, the demesne economy could dominate income from the 1540s onwards. Only 6 per cent of total income came from village rents on noble estates and 29.8 per cent on royal ones in 1551–80. Demesne arable agriculture generated the major share, at between 70 and 80 per cent [195, 197, 199, 204]. By the eighteenth century, profit from the sale of alcohol had become very important, while, as the estates of the Zamoyskis demonstrate, less than 10 per cent of annual gross income came from cash rents. Demesne farming clearly was a commercial success, either because of the sale of grain to foreign markets or through distilling. In the second half of the eighteenth century, estate accounts show that as little as 3 per cent and as much as 85 per cent of gross income derived from alcohol monopolies (*propinacja*); demesne farming represented between 25 and 40 per cent and villagers' rents amounted to a maximum of 40 per cent. However, there were also different patterns [188]. On royal estates in Little Poland, rent payments from the rural population could make up up to 80 per cent of seignorial income [175, 177, 185, 202].

In many estates in the Czech Lands, earnings from cash rents declined to between 10 and 30 per cent of total income by the middle of the sixteenth century. In the sixteenth century fish farming remained important, representing up to 40 per cent of gross income, and the brewing sector started to expand, generating between 25 and 45 per cent of income. In estates specialising in arable demesne farming, this sector contributed up to 30 per cent to seignorial income. Yet there were estates that continued to rely mainly on rent income. In the seventeenth and eighteenth centuries, the demesne sector created between two-thirds and three-quarters of seignorial income. By the mid-eighteenth century, breweries mostly formed the dominant demesne sector in Bohemia, including areas less favourable for arable agriculture, while cash rents represented only between 8 and 13 per cent of income [1, 5, 42, 67, 86]. Brewing was also important in Silesia [162]. In Bohemia, Moravia and Silesia, lords also profited from investment in proto-industrial activities, such as bleacheries, textile trading, textile manufactories or iron and glass works [68, 72, 187]. On Upper Silesian estates, demesne iron mills generated 10 to 17 per cent of gross income after 1740 [196].

The rising income from demesne activities in overall and gross terms cannot be doubted, but it is more difficult to trace its success in real terms, or in terms of modern business statistics such as return on capital or other indicators. A more systematic evaluation will have to wait for future investigation. Available studies in this respect suggest that net profits amounted to between two-fifths and two-thirds of gross income [67, 88, 91, 94, 100, 116, 197].

Does this mean that the commercial demesne economy made all Eastern European nobles rich? To begin with, the survey in this chapter has shown that many estates continued to rely on villagers' rents as their main source of income. In most countries the exten-sion of the demesne economy was accompanied by a consolidation of estate property in the hands of a limited number of large land-owning families (often described as 'magnates' or 'high nobility' in the literature). The majority of estates, however, were of limited size and many of the smaller ones struggled economically. In periods of structural crises in income, such as during the first half of the sixteenth or the second half of the seventeenth century, many smaller estates had to be sold because of high debts. This is not to say that even large magnate families did not incur high debts because of mismanage-ment, because income could not keep pace with enormous increases in expenses or because the expansion of estate property had left them overburdened with debt. Buying new estates or investment in demesnes did not always bring about commercial success. The indebtedness of noble families remained a relatively common phenomenon.

[vii]   Conclusions

A commercial demesne economy was a significant characteristic of demesne lordship, but it did not develop everywhere in East-Central and Eastern Europe, and it also experienced phases of severe con-traction (as in Estonia or Livonia) or was of importance only for a comparatively short duration (in Russia or Moldavia and Wallachia). The growth of demesne farming was not usually based on the expro-priation of tenant land. The extent of the demesne economy and its importance for seignorial income varied considerably according to region and period. When there were demesnes, the sector usually constituted the major share of an estate's income. This pattern existed side by side with others in which rent-based income continued to domi-nate. The demesne economy was also highly adaptable. Authorities were quick to respond to changes in business cycles or if demesne farming turned out to be unprofitable in a certain place, for instance for reasons of scale or soil. Activities in arable or livestock farming were complemented by forestry or by investment in breweries and distilleries, which were supported by seignorial monopoly rights.

Labour rents of villagers are among the consequences of demesne lordship to which the literature devotes most attention. Several factors such as the extent of demesne land or management practices could influence the actual demand for *corvée*. Where heavy labour rents of three days or more per week occurred, these certainly constituted the most significant burden of demesne lordship. As the survey has shown, even in countries with a high share of demesne land and high average labour rent burdens, there were estates that relied on direct management with wage labour. There were also swings over time between the relative importance of labour rents and wage labour.

The general picture that emerges is that the extent of demesne activities, their significance for seignorial income and their organisation of work was more varied and flexible than has previously been presented. This aspect of demesne lordship therefore does not support the idea of a uniform system or of a general serfdom, either.

That the success of demesnes rested on the exploitation of villagers was almost universally accepted in traditional interpretations. It cannot be doubted that any type of ancien régime lordship (including those in Western and Southern Europe) worked on the basis of appropriation of tenant surplus or their work (or both). In East-Central and Eastern Europe, demesne lordship drew on tenant resources by means of labour rents, market monopolies and other forms of rent extraction. Yet it is also important to acknowledge that the actual extent of these patterns varied enormously and that villagers should not be regarded as powerless victims. For instance, demesne expansion did not occur primarily at the expense of tenant land. Tenants had considerable autonomy in dealing with labour rents, including various strategies and forms of action that helped to avoid them altogether. Seignorial market monopolies could not undermine the commercial orientation of the tenant economy (see Chapter 5, Section ii). These are but a few doubts that have raised in more recent research and that justify the question, originally put in the context of research on Brandenburg [116], of whether the rise of the demesne economy may in general have been more symbiotic with than destructive of the tenant economy. The effects on the welfare of the rural population thus remain open for more detailed investigation and re-assessment (see Chapter 5, Sections iii and iv).

5 A General Backwardness?

[i] Introduction

Did the demesne economy system cause long-term economic stagnation and backwardness in the rural economy and obstruct economic development [11, 47]? There has been an astonishing degree of agreement that it did in many approaches to research, irrespective of their theoretical background (cf. Chapters 1 and 3). According to their verdicts, (i) demesne and tenant agriculture were largely traditional, market averse, backward and characterised by low yields and lack of productivity, which led to a stagnation in overall income; (ii) seignorial interests and regulations such as mobility restrictions or monopolies undermined the economic activities of the rural population; and (iii) urban development and the growth of crafts and proto-industries remained very limited because of demesne lordship.

Studies claim that the use of labour rents made early modern commercial demesne farming less productive and efficient than agriculture based on wage labour [29, 176] and that the system was slow to change from traditional field systems to more efficient forms of cultivation. For an empirical foundation, the literature refers to the stagnation and decline of yields in Poland between the sixteenth and the early eighteenth centuries [160, 205]. It is argued that labour rents reduced the workforce available for tenant households, preventing them from intensifying their economy and, like seignorial monopolies, reducing their market participation. While empirical results question these conclusions and emphasise differentiation, successful regional specialisation and market participation of demesne and tenant farming, researchers have failed to develop a decisive counter-argument to these traditional meta-narratives. As mentioned in Chapter 3, export and domestic market demand worked together. Population growth, urbanisation, increasing economic specialisation, the rise of proto-industrial regions and market integration represented powerful stimuli for commercial agricultural production on the demesne and tenant level. The picture of a generally low standard of living among rural households has also been scrutinised [8, 67, 72, 106, 116, 119, 122, 130, 166, 201]. As a result, a new assessment of agricultural change in individual Eastern European countries during the seventeenth, eighteenth and nineteenth centuries is an important agenda for future research.

[ii]   The Economic Consequences of Demesne Lordship

Research has produced an abundance of data on grain yields. These illustrate the main point raised in this chapter; that is, the variation of productivity in the agricultural sector as opposed to the assumed uniformity of high yields in the West and low ones in the East, as suggested by computed aggregate averages. This has been emphasised by other scholars, but with little apparent effect (see for difficulties of comparison [83, 205]). Thus, where possible, the data in Table 5.1 are arranged to show the range of (average) yields rather than only averages. As in most other respects, more evidence exists for demesne agriculture than for tenant farms and smallholdings. While the general assertion that tenant farming must have achieved higher yields than demesne farming rests on a number of plausible assumptions such as higher labour and capital inputs, empirical proof of the productivity advantage is rare.

While aggregate grain yields in East-Central and Eastern Europe are close to the averages of early modern Europe, they lagged behind the most productive regions of the European North-West [61]. Values of 1 : 3 or lower as occasionally reported in the literature as proof for the weakness of Eastern European agriculture [61, 63] look exceptional, and when they occurred often seemed to affect oat (usually sown on the least fertile land). Even in North-Western Europe, yields varied enormously between regions [8] and this presents an even larger problem with regard to the enormous size and environmental diversity of Eastern Europe. A good example is the contradictory nature of a vast array of yield figures compiled in dozens of empirical studies from different areas of the

Table 5.1 Yield ratios in arable farming in East-Central and Eastern Europe, c.1550–1820

Region	Period			
	1500s	**1600s**	**1700s**	**1800s**
Belorussia/Lithuania	1 : 5	1 : 5	—	—
Bohemia/Moravia	1 : 5–6	1 : 4–10 Rye 1 : 2–7.1 Wheat 1 : 2.6–7.1 Barley 1 : 3.5–7.7 Oats 1 : 2.1–7	Tenant 1 : 6	—
Brandenburg	—	—	1 : 4–6 Rye 1 : 4–7.2 Barley 1 : 5–9 Oats 1 : 4–5	—
East Prussia	Rye 1 : 3.5 Wheat 1 : 5 Barley 1 : 4 Oats 1 : 2.8	Rye 1 : 3.5 Wheat 1 : 5 Barley 1 : 3.3–5.5	—	—
Estonia	—	1 : 2.9–5.5 Rye 1 : 3.5–4.6 Barley 1 : 3.5–4.6 Oats 1 : 2.2–1 : 5–2	1 : 4–6	1 : 4.2–5
Hungary	1 : 4 Wheat 1 : 1.2–4.3 Barley 1 : 1.3–5.1 Oats 1 : 1.1–5.1	1 : 4 Rye 1 : 1.4–7.7 Wheat 1 : 1.4–5.9	Rye 1 : 1.1–12.1 Wheat 1 : 1.4–14.7 Barley 1 : 1.1–7.6 Oats 1 : 1.1–10	—

Latvia	1:5.5 Rye 1:3.7–5.6 Barley 1:4–6.1 Oats 1:2–3.4	Rye 1:4.3–4.7 Barley 1:2.8–5.4	Rye 1:6 Barley 1:6.5 Oats 1:5	Rye 1:6 Barley 1:5 Oats 1:4
Livonia	1:3–5 Rye 1:4.7	1:4.3	1:4.8–7.1	1:5.2
Mecklenburg	1:3.9–4 Rye 1:3.3–6.4 Barley 1:3–5.6 Oats 1:2.7–4.7	Barley 1:4.4–4.9	1:5–8	—
Poland (Great Poland, Mazovia, Little Poland)	Tenant Rye 1:5 Wheat 1:5 Barley 1:6.2 Oats 1:4.8 Demesne 1:5.1 1:4.3–6.44 Rye 1:3.2–5 Wheat 1:4.3–7.6 Barley 1:4.5–8.0 Oats 1:1.8–7	1:4.4–6.11 Rye 1:2.5–5.7 Wheat 1:4.4–7.6 Barley 1:4.7–6 Oats 1:2.4–6.4	1:3.5–6 Rye 1:4.8–5.9 Wheat 1:6.2–8.4 Barley 1:6.8–8.8 Oats 1:3.1–5.8	—

(continued)

97

Table 5.1 Continued

Region	Period			
	1500s	1600s	1700s	1800s
Pomerania	Rye 1 : 3–11 Barley 1 : 3–6 Oats 1 : 2–4	1 : 4–5	1 : 4–6	—
Russia central/non-*chernozem*	1 : 3–5	—	1 : 3 Rye 1 : 3.1–4.65 Wheat 1 : 3–4.9	—
Russia *chernozem*	—	—	1 : 4.5–6	1 : 3.3–6.2
Schleswig-Holstein	—	Rye 1 : 7 Barley 1 : 4–6.1	Rye 1 : 6.7 Wheat 1 : 6.5	Barley 1 : 5.5–7.3 Oats 1 : 3.2–6.7
Silesia	1 : 4.1	—	Rye 1 : 3.5–5.2 Wheat 1 : 4.4–6 Barley 1 : 4.2–5.8 Oats 1 : 2.7–4.3	Rye 1 : 5 Wheat 1 : 7.5 Barley 1 : 6 Oats 1 : 3.7
Upper Lusatia	Rye 1 : 3.3	Rye 1 : 2.4–3.5 Barley 1 : 2.4–3.2	Rye 1 : 4 Barley 1 : 3–4.4	—

Sources: [56, 63, 67, 100, 130, 145, 152, 183, 197, 199, 205, 215].

Polish Commonwealth, of which only a small sample is represented in Table 5.1. Low yields are typically associated with Russia, but in fact, Russian *chernozem* yields in particular were rather high [214]. Some areas of demesne lordship abandoned traditional field systems as early as the sixteenth century in favour of more innovative techniques (see Section iii), which had the potential to increase yields substantially. A lower agricultural labour input, less intensive land use and a range of other income sources from forestry, fishing or hunting may have resulted in relatively limited attention to arable agriculture and comparatively smaller yields [61, 214, 221]. To highlight some of these problems, Table 5.2 summarises systematic references to high yields in the literature.

Apart from these observations linked to particular regions or specific forms of farm management, variation between years also indicates that high yields were not exceptional. For instance, Eastern Pomeranian princely estates show overall average yields around 1 : 4 or 1 : 5, but varied between 1 : 2.5 and 1 : 9 in the first decades of the seventeenth century [192]. Relatively high yields are usually associated with agriculture in Bohemia and Moravia, where 25 to 50 per cent of the yields analysed were higher than 1 : 4 in 1500–1750 [67, 83, 205]. Between 20 and 40 per cent of the yields measured for rye, wheat and barley in various regions of Poland were greater than 1 : 4 in the period 1500–1650. In 1750–1800, between 15 and 60 per cent were higher than 1 : 6 [205]. Yields of 1 : 7 to 1 : 20 are recorded too often to be regarded as a mere coincidence of weather conditions. For sixteenth- and seventeenth-century Polish demesnes, maximum yields were 1 : 17 for wheat, 1: 12 for rye and1 : 17 for barley; for tenants the figures were 1 : 10.5 for wheat and 1 : 20 for barley. There was a strong increase in arable yields during the second half of the eighteenth century [205]. Maximum yields in seventeenth- and eighteenth-century Schleswig-Holstein were 1 : 12. Yields higher than 1 : 8 can be considered good in European comparison for the eighteenth century, even if the maximum, represented by examples from Dutch regions, was higher than 1 : 20, and the average for England and the Low Countries more than 1 : 11 in 1800 [61, 130, 159].

Evidence is also available for different measures of yields (Table 5.3). The accounts of one Bohemian tenant farmer in 1729–32 show that grain yields per hectare (for a mix of wheat and mainly rye and barley) was 658 kg or approximately 11.41 hl [77]. For the period

Table 5.2 References to high yields, c.1500–1860

Date	Region	Yield	Note
c.1500–80	Poland	1 : 7–8	Noble demesnes
c.1550–1620	Bohemia	1 : 10–12	Fertile regions
c.1550–1620	Bohemia	1 : 7–9	Medium soil
1600–1800	Schleswig-Holstein	1 : 6–7	
1650–99	Estonia	1 : 6–8 (norm), 1 : 9–11 (peak)	
1660–1720	Little Poland	>1 : 4	Yields in 19 out of 34 demesnes
1681–99	Estonia	1 : 12	Barley and oats, island of Ösel Wiek
c.1730	Bohemia	1 : 6	Account of a tenant farm
1750–1800	Brandenburg	1 : 18–24	Drained areas, rivers Oder/Warta
1750–1800	Holstein	1 : 20–30	
1760–1800	Little Poland	1 : 8.9–11.5	Highest averages of particular demesnes
c.1770	Lithuania	1 : 10	Expected wheat and rye yields, royal demesnes, fertile land
1797	Pomerania	1 : 24	Rye yields, island of Rügen
c.1800	Russia	1 : 10	Slash-and-burn cultivation
1811–60	Russia	1 : 6.2	*Chernozem* estate, rye

Sources: [63, 77, 94, 100, 130, 184, 197, 215].

1600–50, average grain yields of tenant farms in Mazovia were estimated to amount to 120 to 180 Gdańsk bushels per hide (c.214.3 to 341.2 kg per hectare), with a maximum of 541 bushels (966.1 kg per hectare) [204]. The data thus provide a firm basis for a reconsideration of the hypothesis of a general 'backwardness' in terms of agricultural yields.

Agricultural techniques and field systems in East-Central and Eastern Europe were more varied and dynamic than is generally assumed. Research so far has been predominantly preoccupied with

Table 5.3   Estimates of yields per hectare land (in kg or hl)

Period	Area	Yield (hl)	Yield (kg)	Note
1500–1600	Europe	–	400–500	Wheat and rye
	Poland		320–480	–
1550–1695	East Prussia	–	700–760	Rye/barley, 11 demesnes
1580–1655	Poland	8.2–9.6	504–600	Demesnes, Great Poland
1590–1610	Bohemia	–	350–1650	Rye demesnes of 2 estates
1590–1610	Bohemia	–	650–2000	Barley demesnes of 2 estates
c.1600	Eastern Pomerania	–	612	–
1688–90	Lower Silesia	–	640–940	Oat and barley/rye
c.1700	Mecklenburg	–	500–600	–
1700–1800	Bohemia	–	830–1200	Wheat demesnes
1700–1800	Bohemia	–	700–980	Rye demesnes
1700–1800	Bohemia	–	600–1010	Barley demesnes
1700–1800	Bohemia	–	400–860	Oat demesnes
1759	Denmark	–	1474	–
c.1800	East Prussia	–	780–1020	Rye/oat/wheat/barley demesnes
c.1800	East Prussia	–	900–1400	Rye/wheat demesnes
c.1800	Lower Silesia	–	885–1030	Rye/oat/barley demesnes
c.1800	Brandenburg	–	1130–1370	Rye/oat demesnes
c.1800	Brandenburg	–	1200–1440	Barley/wheat demesnes
1811–60	Russia	12–19.3	–	Rye/oat

Sources: [60, 61, 67, 74, 170, 174, 192, 193, 197, 200].

the broad eighteenth-century reforms and amelioration measures. There are a number of individual and more structural examples for other periods as well. The management of princely estates in various countries throughout the early modern period repeatedly undertook structural reforms that await assessment in this respect [98, 140, 140]. For instance, there were systematic efforts to improve dairy farming in demesnes in the Duchy of Western Pomerania with the help of Dutch specialists in the 1560s [145], in Mecklenburg, in Schleswig-Holstein [140] and in seventeenth-century Courland. In Brandenburg, Schleswig-Holstein and Poland, contacts with the Dutch Republic during the seventeenth and eighteenth centuries led to the immigration of specialists, changes in field drainage systems and the claiming of large new areas for agricultural use. Dairy farming – the farms were appropriately called 'Dutch' (*Holländereien*) – improved considerably. Arable techniques display similar flexibility. For instance, summer fields on sixteenth-century Brandenburg demesnes were ploughed four times and drainage was improved [106]. Demesne lords or their managers continuously reviewed the possibilities of improvement. After the Northern Wars, yields of Livonian demesnes were improved by increasing livestock numbers to enable more intensive manuring. Estates in eighteenth-century Bohemia systematically increased livestock numbers to raise arable productivity [94, 140, 179].

During the later fifteenth and sixteenth centuries, changes in Mecklenburg and parts of Pomerania brought about a gradual abandonment of earlier cultivation systems without regular fallow and the adoption of new methods. Tenant and demesne agriculture introduced a division into four and five fields (which would mean a maximum fallow of only 25 or 20 per cent of the soil) and an elaborate system of crop rotation. In some areas, seven-field rotation was adopted. A key element was that these techniques were adapted freely to local conditions. Their implementation made changes in field layout necessary. For instance, separation and consolidation of demesne land was common in Pomerania after 1650 [105, 192].

As early as the seventeenth century, princely demesne farms in East Prussia used four- to six-field rotation. Among eleven cases investigated, two used a four-field rotation and one worked without regular fallow, dividing the arable fields into six separate entities. The fallow was partly used for growing summer crops [193]. Four field-systems were not entirely unknown in sixteenth-century Polish demesnes either [197], and were introduced on seventeenth-century Courland princely estates along with better ploughing practices, more intensive weeding and improved drainage. Following this, individual estates reported yields of 1 : 9. However, many an improvement or investment was then wrecked by the impact of the Northern War from 1655–60 and farming had to start again from scratch. Four- and five-field rotation also spread into eighteenth-century Bohemia [74].

In Mecklenburg, the introduction of the so-called *Koppelwirtschaft* in the later seventeenth and early eighteenth centuries, which gave rise to a new wave of expropriation of tenant land, represents a case of a more structural innovation under demesne lordship. It was made easier by the abundance of deserted tenant farmland after the Thirty Years' War and spread into Western Pomerania during the eighteenth century. Separation of demesne and tenant land on princely demesnes in the Duchy of Mecklenburg-Strelitz was completed after 1780, often carried out by seizing tenant land and resettling farmers on other plots [105, 128, 147].

The origins of *Koppelwirtschaft* can be found in systematic innovations in sixteenth-century Schleswig-Holstein demesne farming. It spread so quickly that by 1600 most estates had already introduced this system, which had to do with specialisation in animal husbandry. By contrast, until 1730 only a small minority of tenant farmers had used it, although in some parts of Schleswig tenant farms had already introduced it. Demesne lords occasionally tried to prevent a change in tenant field systems, because they feared that it could harm their access to open village resources. Tenant farmers in demesne areas normally used four- or five-field systems from the sixteenth and seventeenth centuries [105, 140, 148]. The decisive feature of Holstein *Koppelwirtschaft* was that the traditional separation of arable and pastoral land was abolished and a convertible system was used [105, 140, 147]. Mecklenburg and Schleswig-Holstein became two of the most productive agricultural regions in Germany. The adapted system was called *mecklenburgische Schlagwirtschaft* and came to dominate Mecklenburg demesne agriculture during the eighteenth century [105, 147].

In the Electorate of Brandenburg, the spread of *Koppelwirtschaft* after 1650 was accompanied by separating tenant and demesne land and consolidating demesnes. Weak property rights were an advantage in forcing tenants into exchanging parcels. The estate of Plattenburg-Wilsnack introduced forms of the system during the seventeenth century [135], although greater progress was made during the second half of the eighteenth century, when innovations were adapted to regional conditions. Improvements of arable fields were accompanied by other measures concerning pastures, which increased their value and yield [118, 122, 130]. Princely estates that adopted these improvements achieved the highest grain yields, with values up to 1 : 19 and 1 : 24 (1 : 7 on average). Due to changes in convertible husbandry, the quantity of seed applied to a largely unchanged acreage increased threefold in Stavenow between 1719 and 1809 and yields increased by 50 per cent [116, 117]. This also made possible a strong increase in areas used for growing wheat and barley, which yielded higher profits because of particularly large price increases. These changes demanded major investments accompanied by works to improve and extend existing stables and related buildings.

Tenant farms adopted these forms of intensive farming during the later eighteenth century. Four-field rotation was common and there was also a shift to wheat and barley cultivation. New techniques continued to be employed on demesne fields, even after they had been leased to tenant farmers [130]. Tenants sometimes adopted more progressive field systems long before the eighteenth century. In several Mecklenburg and Pomeranian estates, villages using traditional three-field rotation were the minority during the sixteenth century. By 1700, not a single village used the three-field system in the Pomeranian estate of Barth; 40 per cent of the villages did not have any field divisions, and most of the others used a system of five fields. This may have had to do with a shift towards cereals for animal husbandry, possibly caused by the necessity to keep more draught animals for labour rents [147]. Communities made the necessary large-scale investments. In the early 1780s, the villagers of Zehlendorf put 1,000 *taler*, which they had received in compensation for losing part of the common pasture, into draining additional land. Other capital came from investments from the wealthy citizens of nearby Berlin, who bought some of the tenant farms and leased them to locals. The development was completed by a new noble lord, who was a supporter of agrarian innovation. The consolidation and separation of the village's demesne and tenant fields, which he initiated, met with some resistance [149]. As this conflict occurred in the context of successful other innovations carried out in the same village, it illustrates that occasional resistance is no evidence of villagers' alleged traditionalism, but very much to do with specific harm expected from individual measures. Even contemporaries noted the adoption of new techniques among tenant farmers around Berlin and depicted these farmers as 'extremely well educated' [130]. In several regions of the Brandenburg Altmark, villagers had partitioned the commons and consolidated their holdings long before 1800. With yields of 1 : 12–16 they harvested two to three times as much as the assumed average [130]. The demands of the fast-growing city of Berlin proved an important incentive. The city of Gdańsk and the grain export trade provided the same stimulus for intensification and improvement among tenant farmers in Royal Prussia around 1600 [179]. Recent surveys also contest the idea of a long-term stagnation of the Russian rural economy [223, 225].

The spread of agrarian innovations in East-Central Europe was a long-term process (just like elsewhere) and was also accompanied by processes of commercialisation and regional specialisation, in extreme cases even commercial monocultures [135, 140, 153, 159]. There is no reason to assume a stagnation of agricultural development over the early modern period. Key elements of the changes were part of a European-wide trend of reforms in the eighteenth century, such as the strengthening of tenants' property rights, the improvement of agricultural land, and domestic settlement and colonisation movements to increase the agricultural area in use. In many countries, this initiated a pronounced growth in agricultural output. For instance, in Russia alone 21.4 million hectares of forests were cleared and cultivated land increased from 20 per cent to 31 per cent of the total between 1696 and 1796, an increase much stronger than simultaneous population growth. The use of new and improved tools and techniques spread along with these changes [106, 122, 124, 222].

In recent years, the analysis of estate management has come into focus, which, especially in the case of larger estates, relied on professional personnel, led by a manager (steward; German *Amtmann, Hauptmann*). Much has been made of the alleged general carelessness of demesne management, but when in seignorial accounts demesne lords and stewards painfully followed every single penny that they thought they were entitled to receive from demesnes or villages, this seems a questionable view. Studies are now challenging the traditional account of an inflexible, old-fashioned and largely unprofitable regime (had it not been for labour rents), averse to investment and innovation. Russian landowners may have been unwilling to invest in agricultural improvements on their estates, but they did put large sums into developing manufacture and industry [219]. Polish research indicates that in the sixteenth century a hide of demesne land yielded a profit 15 times higher than the profit (via rent) from a tenant hide, and regards demesne lords as 'rational manager(s)' [176, 180, 197]. Research on the demesne economy in sixteenth- and early seventeenth-century Bohemia and Moravia refers to innovative seignorial management and investment behaviour, as elsewhere geared to extending demesne operations or increasing revenue by other means. Considerable sums were used to buy additional property [67]. Reforms in the vast princely estates in various countries were driven by the necessity to raise income to cover mushrooming state expenses. This did not only involve shifts between direct management and leasing, but also led to an overhaul of management procedures and accounting practices [145, 192].

To make optimal use of the available labour, Estonian lords reviewed work processes and assigned land according to the size of the household labour available. As soon as sufficient numbers of tenants were available, demesnes were systematically extended [100]. Substantial investments were necessary to rebuild and improve the commercial demesne economy during the second half of the seventeenth century. In the process, many nobles lost their estates, because their means ran out. When agricultural prices rose in the eighteenth century, investments were not only earmarked for an extension of demesne farming (which means extensive growth), but also for improving soils, techniques and equipment, which enhanced productivity. The introduction of *Koppel-* and *Schlagwirtschaft* in Mecklenburg required considerable investment to change field structures, build flexible field divisions and increase the number of livestock. Especially in the beginning, lords may have faced difficulties raising the necessary capital [105, 147]. They were also flexible in terms of wage and forced labour and in leasing demesne farms, when conditions changed so that direct management became less attractive. A close connection to grain price development and a trend towards optimising demesne production has also been concluded for demesne estates in Scania [91]. Dynamic developments and innovation in noble and princely estates became particularly obvious during the eighteenth century. The detailed financial transactions of lords need to be analysed more closely in future to come to a full picture of management and investment practices [106, 116, 122, 130].

Stavenow in Brandenburg provides a snapshot of these points. The initial growth of demesne investment between 1520 and 1540 saw the manor house rebuilt, the construction of two new demesne farms and two mills, purchases of additional fields and the move of a river bed. In 1680–91 alone the lord invested 23 000 *taler* (not including his residential building), a considerable sum given that gross income from the estate was 6500 *taler* per annum in the late 1740s. In addition, rebuilding and re-equipping 46 tenant farms destroyed after 1650 cost nearly 6000 *taler*. These investments and improvements raised the estate's value considerably [116]. While the sixteenth-century increase in seignorial income was largely built on scale – that is, on the expansion of the demesnes' acreage – productivity-enhancing measures were part and parcel of demesne farming in the eighteenth century. The changes relied on skilled management with an eye to market developments and the adoption of innovative agricultural techniques, resulting in a significant increase in income and also in estate values. William Hagen concludes that Brandenburg demesne lords transformed themselves into 'aristocratic entrepreneurs' over the long term [116].

In short, demesnes could turn out to become 'a highly profitable enterprise' [91] not only because of extra-economic coercion. Since the late Middle Ages, noble lords often had tried to establish a professional management system as a means to this end. They introduced detailed written accounting, instructions and administration, but also control [94, 219]. It is true that such an apparatus was probably missing on the many small estates with a few tenants and a single demesne farm (if any), but in such cases the lords were probably in a better situation to keep track of developments themselves.

The original argument of the low productivity of demesne farming also rested on the assumption of lower labour productivity of labour rents compared to agricultural wage labour. This idea, originating from a brief remark in Adam Smith's *Wealth of Nations* – an author who, by the way, shared his enlightened contemporaries' prejudices and likened the fate of Eastern European villagers to outright 'slavery' – has so often been repeated in the literature that it has become a truism. However, a general empirical test of this assumption is still missing; what little empirical evidence we have cannot be regarded as very sound due to problems of documentation and analysis. Although many lords and estate managers thought that labour rents were less productive [116], overall contemporaries were divided in their assessment. This ambivalence may have been due to an attempt to save costs or avoid at least part of the initial investment required, such as for draught animals or equipment. In estates with labour rents, wage expenses for the demesnes were as small as 2 per cent of gross income around 1600. Those without labour rents had expenses for wages of 12 to 18 per cent of income (see Chapter 4, Section vi). If certain institutional arrangements made possible the use of both wage labour and labour rents, lords would choose between the two or occasionally shift the balance. In general, a mixed system prevailed (see Chapter 4, Section iv).

When innovations failed or were not adopted everywhere, structural conditions may have been among the reasons. They would make little sense if they rendered necessary increased labour inputs that could not be met in periods when many tenant farms were deserted. The relative abundance of land in particular regions, such as in Livonia, determined that certain areas were only used extensively for arable agriculture. With vast desertions caused by the Northern Wars, land reserves were sown only irregularly and only gradually included in continuous arable farming. As demesne arable acreage often increased faster than livestock, manure was in short supply on demesne farms and prohibited a more intensive use of the fields [93, 94, 100]. The introduction of *Koppelwirtschaft* in demesne agriculture in Mecklenburg met with villagers' resistance for good reasons. Tenants faced losing their farms and becoming mere smallholders or cottagers. The attempted consolidation of demesne farms in Holstein threatened traditional pasture rights. Consequently, villagers not only refused to render the necessary labour rents but also tore down new fences, filled new ditches and had their cattle graze these fields [112, 130].

Traditional accounts refer to the lack of market orientation and limited economic possibilities of tenant agriculture as well as being market averse as other negative consequences of demesne lordship. These two aspects must be separated. While the system could definitely be harmful, for instance due to the lack of secure property rights, the burdens of labour rents (loss of labour and the depreciation of the necessary tools and draught power; see e.g. [60, 148]) and the extension of seignorial market production supported by monopolies and privileges, studies available for Brandenburg, Silesia, Poland, Hungary, Bohemia, Moravia and Russia show economic independence, successful market participation, taking advantage of market swings and price movements and a high degree of market involvement of tenant farmers and smallholders, some of whom grew wealthy in the process [34, 72, 84, 85, 108, 116, 119, 124, 135, 153, 155, 170, 178, 210, 212].

The extensive use of tenants' plough teams for labour rents meant that at least some of the tenant farms were large enough to maintain additional draught animals or farmhands to carry out the necessary obligations and work their own farms. When tenants defended their customary rights to land in Holstein in 1706–7, they claimed that they could only render heavy labour rents as long as it was guaranteed that they held farms large enough to supply them [34, 112]. With limited land to feed and pasture their herds in any case, the necessary resources to keep additional draught power would mean a reduction in other necessary livestock, such as cattle. It was estimated that for each extra pair of horses a tenant farm could have kept three cattle or twelve sheep. Alternatively, they shifted from using horse power to oxen for their labour rents. Due to the seasonal character of agriculture, labour rents were demanded at a time when workers were most needed on tenant farms as well. The amount of capital and farm equipment shows that tenants were prepared for this (see Section iv) [14, 214, 225].

With regard to the second aspect, more than enough evidence is already available to demonstrate that villagers seized the opportunities opened up by the commercial infrastructure. They were thus far from market-averse 'peasants' as they were presented by particular scholarly traditions, which argued that this was caused by demesne lordship [44, 120, 122, 130]. In Poland and Bohemia, sixteenth-century conditions are regarded as favourable for tenant farmers despite the rise of demesne farming and increasing obligations. The rise in grain prices increased the incomes of those regularly selling harvest surpluses on the market, while fixed rents decreased in real terms and tax increases remained limited for the time being. The monetary value of the harvest net of seed of Silesian fullholders is estimated to have grown more than fourfold between 1500 and 1600 [34, 66, 82, 83, 166, 168, 178, 186, 201]. When grain trade restrictions were in place, such as in Livonia, farmers compensated for this by selling other products such as flax and hemp. But even in this region, tenant farmers participated directly in the market with large amounts of grain, as there were frequent complaints about independent direct marketing at Baltic ports [94, 98, 101]. Tenants also profited from growing market demand and rising grain prices during the eighteenth century [116, 120].

Tenant farmers and smallholders were bound to develop market activities and acquire detailed knowledge about market conditions. Close market links were helped by the fact that town monopolies had been undermined. Hartmut Harnisch developed a model of the economy of tenant farmers in demesne lordship according to which intensive market orientation was a consequence of the structure of rents and dues. As monetary and product rents were relatively low, because labour rents were high, tenants retained a greater share of the production to be sold [119]. Even if the market quota of Brandenburg tenant farmers had only remained constant between 1766 and 1801, their income would have doubled due to the rise in grain prices over the period. When landlords increased cash rents by 10 to 20 per cent towards the end of the century, this far from matched the additional income resulting from growth in grain prices [118, 120]. The swift introduction of new crops on tenant farms, such as tobacco or potatoes, or product specialisation in barley and wheat, also had to do with the recognition of market changes.

The traditional argument that the prevailing nature of the economy was agrarian and that there was stagnation in the urban and secondary sectors has also been criticised since the 1950s. Proto-industrial specialisation in some areas has long been acknowledged, but was seen as isolated to conditions of demesne lordship without the full development of a demesne economy (for instance areas in Bohemia, Moravia, Central Russia, Upper Lusatia, Silesia and the Balkan territories of the Ottoman Empire) and of ultimate failure (for instance Silesia or Little Poland). However, areas with proto-industrial production can be found in almost all territories and the development was compatible even with a fully developed demesne economy. The main sectors were textile (linen and wool, later cotton) and iron manufacturing in areas of the Czech Lands, the northern parts of the Hungarian Kingdom (Slovakia), Poland–Lithuania, Russia and Sweden. Demesne lords sometimes participated as entrepreneurs in proto-industrial activities as owners of or investors in textile manufactories or iron mills [8, 68,72, 212]; they also realised that they could profit from the successful participation of villagers in proto-industrial production and trade [68, 72, 210].

Substantial proportions of the rural population were active outside arable agriculture. Among their activities were animal husbandry in various forms and different work related to forestry and fishing, along the coasts but also on inland rivers and lakes. Many of these people enjoyed lower burdens or more liberties in terms of mobility or labour rents than those owning tenant farms or smallholdings.

The most important conclusion to be drawn is that villagers engaged in markets regularly and were able to make independent decisions about production and economic strategies, even in areas of demesne lordship and a commercial demesne economy [44, 108, 124, 215, 225]. This questions the general assumption that subject or serf farming was generally backward and traditional. Evidently, there was a range of possible seignorial influences on villagers' households, and these need to be studied in their respective contexts and for their specific effects. They were more likely to restrict villagers in certain aspects rather than generally prevent a successful market orientation. Due to the powers that some lords used, economic relations in rural societies could be asymmetric [44], but a widespread interference of lords in the economy of tenant households on a day-to-day basis cannot be observed.

Re-assessment is also necessary with respect to the general 'backwardness' of East-Central and Eastern Europe as a result of demesne lordship and the demesne economy. The conclusions of William Hagen, for instance, demonstrate this approach for Brandenburg-Prussia: '[T]he rise of the Junker estates neither ruined the east-Elbian villages nor prevented the absolutist state, working in alliance with the educated and propertied bourgeoisie, from launching Brandenburg-Prussia successfully on the path of nineteenth-century industrialization' [117].

[iii]   Villagers' Living Standards

An analysis of the economic success of tenant farming has to rely on a number of assumptions such as harvest yields or servant wages. There is some difficulty in comparing the results, which usually refer to a certain regional or chronological context in terms of wage and price levels. Similar uncertainties must be assumed for the level of rents and taxes. Although we are quite well informed about the prescribed burdens, we often lack data, for example, on how many days of labour rents tenants actually rendered. Rents in cash and kind, though as a rule rather small in comparison to Western Europe, could vary enormously between one village and the next. By the seventeenth and eighteenth centuries, state taxes had become a considerable drain on rural household income, for instance in Denmark, Brandenburg-Prussia, Sweden or the Habsburg Monarchy, but less so in Poland. Military conscription was to household labour 'next to death [...] probably the worst calamity' [78, 80, 95, 214, 220]. Strong grain price increases over the same period would ease the burden of rents and taxes [116].

With relatively modest assumptions on grain yields, half farm-holdings in areas of Little Poland would regularly be forced to compensate for a shortfall in grain, while a fullholding farm would dispose of a surplus of less than 10 per cent of the annual harvest (see Table 5.4) [181].

If we were to assume a yield of 175 *korec* (that is, a ratio of 1 : 4) or even more per hide, then half a holding would also provide a net surplus, while a full farm would achieve a surplus of 30 per cent of the harvest. In Mazovia, smallholders who tended a quarter of a full farm would only produce a third to two-thirds of their annual grain demand. Half holdings (c.8.5 hectares in this region) would be fully self-sufficient under the condition of a higher average yield (but incur a shortfall of a third of consumption and rent needs at a lower average yield), while fullholders (16.8 hectares or 41.5 acres)

Table 5.4 Grain balance of tenant farms in Little Poland (district of Sandomierz), 1606 (in *korec*) and Mazovia (Płock episcopal property), 1600–50 (in Gdańsk bushels)

	Little Poland		**Mazovia**	
	Half hide	**1 hide**	**Half hide**	**1 hide**
Harvest	65	130	60–90	120–180
Seed	22	44	22.5	45
Household consumption	49	57	50	62
Rents	10.5	21	10.25–13.25	20.5–25.5
Balance	−16.5	8	−22.75/+4.25	−7.5/+46.5

Notes: 1 *korec* = c.36kg; 1 Gdańsk bushel (average all cereals) = c.30 kg.
Sources: [181, 204].

would either have a negligible deficit or a considerable surplus of 25.8 per cent of the total harvest (c.1400 kg of grain). Another, much more favourable estimate for the period 1500–1600 puts the grain surplus at 4000 kg for full and 1500 kg for half holdings in Poland (Table 5.5, example 2) [166, 201]. To make up for a possible short-fall, tenants often used land from abundant reserves in addition to their holdings. Sometimes this was leased officially, but often it was concealed from seignorial authorities, from whose documentation we usually derive our information [201].

Data based on tithes from tenant farms in five Hungarian counties in the second half of the sixteenth century show that on average between 31.5 and 52.9 per cent of the grain harvest was marketed and between 53.9 and 57.6 per cent of wine production. The production patterns of the wealthiest 10 to 20 per cent of tenant farmers reveal falling grain production and rising wine cultivation in 1549–98. Total market income (including animal husbandry) for the biggest tenant farms was 120 *gulden* per annum (more than 100 *reichstaler* or 2.5 kg of silver). This would mean that it was worth more than two years' of wages for an English day labourer in 1590 and must be interpreted in the context of lower price levels in Hungary [153, 159]. Individual accounts of farms in the hand of townsmen in eighteenth-century Bohemia reveal a market quota of between 40 and 45 per cent of the annual gross harvest. For a holding of 20 hectares, this equalled between 53 and 73 hectolitres of grain [78]. Assuming minimal yield ratios, a full tenant farm in Brandenburg Prignitz produced a net surplus of 74 bushels of grain per year according to a 1649 estimate (one bushel was 40–45 kg of rye) [113, 116]. Even in the famine year of 1770, Boitzenburg farmers marketed 71.3 per cent of their wheat and 32.3 per cent of their barley harvest. Only most of the rye and oats was retained for consumption (13.5 and 6.6 per cent was sold), which gives a total market quota of 20.8 per cent [118]. Against this, the marketable surplus of a typical farm on a Russian *barshchina* estate looks very small. In part, this can be explained by the smaller average size of tenant farms (about 22 acres). From a total harvest of c.43 quintals of predominantly rye and oats, 3–4 quintals were used for taxes and monetary rents and the rest was more than enough for the household consumption of 6–7 people, although it left only a small proportion for sale [214]. Marketing quotas have been found to be up to 20 per cent of gross harvests in the eighteenth and early nineteenth centuries in Estonia, Eastern Prussia, Silesia and Brandenburg [96].

Table 5.5 Household budget models

Example 1: Tenant farm, half a hide, Poland c.1550–1600 (grain balance in kg, monetary value in *grosz*)

Income/expenditure	kg/*grosz*
Harvest net of tithe	3684.8
Seed	784
Rent in kind	280.8
Consumption	1908
Sale	712
Revenue from sale	c.278
Tax	16
Rent	24
Surplus	238

Source: [166].

Example 2: Money income of model tenant farms in Poland, 1501–10 and 1591–1600 (in *złoty*)

Year	Money income	Purchasing power in *ellen* of textiles
Fullholding (one hide)		
1501–10	13–15	16–18
1591–1600	53–61	42–9
Holding of half a hide		
1501–10	4–6	5.6–6.3
1591–1600	16–24	14.8–17.2

Source: [201].

Example 3: Tenant fullholder in Mecklenburg, 1737 (grain balance in *Rostock scheffel*, monetary value in *taler*)

Income/expenditure	Winter (rye)	Summer (barley/oat)
Gross arable yield (winter rye)	144	96/80
Seed	36	24/20
Consumption	48–72	24/20
Net surplus	36–60	48/40

(*continued*)

Table 5.5 Continued

Monetary value of surplus	11.7–19.5	20/10
Income animal husbandry	16.0	
Income cash crops	4.0	
Total monetary income	61.7–69.5	

Expenses	*Taler*
Wages of farmhands	25.2
Wages of day labourers	4.0
Wages of shepherds	2.0
Blacksmith	4.0
Other craft work	3.5
Fish, salt etc.	5.25
Estimate of private consumption	18.8
Tithe for parish priest	1.3
Total expenses	64.0
Profit	c.–2.3/+5.5
Estimated tax	9

Note: Assumed total arable 100 *Rostock scheffel* or 25 hectares; assumed yield ratio 1 : 4.
Source: [128].

Example 4: Fullholding in the Brandenburg village of Warthe, 1766 (in *taler*)

Income/expenditure	*Taler*
Sale of grain/tobacco	79.3
Sale of cattle, sheep, wool, dairy	71.5
Total income	150.8
Household consumption	43.2
Servant wages	20
Other wages	6
Repairs/inventory	17
Taxes	38.8
Seignorial rent	20
Surplus	5.8

Source: [118].

(*continued*)

Table 5.5 Continued

Example 5: Fullholding in the Brandenburg estate of Stavenow (in bushels of rye, barley and oat and *taler* p.a.)

Income/expenditure	Bushels grain/*taler*
Yield net of seed	126
Household consumption	52
Monetary value of net surplus	
1703–52	56
1766–1805	84
Rents and taxes	
1703–52	28
1766–1805	31
Net monetary income	
1703–52	28
1766–1805	53

Source: [116].

Example 6: Average of 46 tenant farms with labour rents in Panker/Schmoel, Holstein, c.1766 (in *reichstaler*)

Income/expenditure	*Reichstaler* (% of total income)
Total income	341.84 (100.0)
Rent	2.93 (0.9)
Labour rents	161.8 (47.3)
Other expenses	154.97 (45.3)
Surplus	22.16 (6.5)

Source: [148].

Example 7: Farm of Jakub Hančl in the village of Lužec, Northern Bohemia, 1728–32 (in *gulden*)

Income/expenditure	*Gulden* (% of expenses)
Grain sales	342
Expenses	
Wages for workers and servants	132 (38.6)
Investment/repairs/ other	59.8 (17.5)

(*continued*)

Table 5.5 Continued

Household consumption	21.5 (6.3)
Mortgage rate	18.7 (5.4)
Taxes	79.3 (23.2)
Seignorial rent	22.6 (6.6)
Church	3.6 (1.1)
Total expenses	337.5 (98.7)
Surplus	4.5 (1.3)

Note: Farm size approx. 17 hectares.
Source: [77].

These examples vary between a modest surplus and a considerable income and sound basis for a livelihood. An approximately balanced budget was also calculated for tenant farms of 23 hectares in the region of Poznań in 1803 [182]. The results are influenced by different assumptions for yields, farm size or rent levels. Regarding wages for servants, the accounts of a Mecklenburg estate in 1743 show that male farmhands caused expenses of more than 43 *taler* a year, of which only a quarter was money wages; 20 *taler* would then cover the cash wages of two male farmhands [116, 127]. It is particularly obvious from examples 1, 2 and 5 to what extent an agricultural boom would boost farm incomes in the sixteenth or eighteenth century. Sixteenth-century grain price inflation, for instance, nearly trebled the purchasing power of agricultural income.

The net income of typical Holstein tenant farms with labour rents in 1766 varied between an annual surplus of 22 *taler* (Table 5.5, example 6) and a deficit of four *taler* [34, 148]. For East Prussia, the annual net monetary income of a full tenant farmer after rents, taxes and expenses for servants was estimated at 40 to 75 *taler* in royal estates and 10 to 60 *taler* in noble ones. A further 30 to 40 *taler* would have to be deducted for the household needs of the farming family, which would leave a small surplus for investment or further consumption. The average net income of a privileged group of tenant farmers (usually without labour rents) could be as much as 90–100 *taler* per year [60]. At Berlin prices in the second half of the eighteenth century, 10 *taler* would have been sufficient on average to buy between 275 and 310 kg of rye, approximately the consumption of one person in a year. The value and capital of Stavenow tenant farms increased considerably between 1720 and 1770 and in one

117

survey 83 per cent of farmhouses were found to be in good condition, with complete livestock and equipment [116].

Household models invariably concentrate on arable agriculture. Additional income came from selling cattle or dairy products, occasional wage labour, fishing, the contributions of children, the sale of wood, market gardening and forestry. According to the example 4 in Table 5.5, income from animal husbandry was nearly as high as from arable farming [43, 116, 118]. For smaller farms in Holstein, income from animal husbandry represented more than a third of total income in 1700 [148]. A substantial Brandenburg dairy farm achieved a net income of 146.5 *taler* around 1770 [120].

Income from occasional employment, labour migration, transport work or trading could be significant. In a Brandenburg village, a widow running a full tenant farm said before a court in 1789 that she hoped to be able to raise 20 *reichstaler* carting timber or wood over the winter [120]. Work in transport also brought some of money for Schleswig-Holstein farmers and lords interfered (without success) because they were afraid that this work would wear out the draught animals needed for labour rents [125]. There was a range of petty or substantial trading opportunities, for instance as intermediaries in proto-industries (yarn or cloth trading), in Upper Lusatia, Lower Silesia, Bohemia, Moravia, regions of Russia and southern Poland [68, 72, 210, 212]. In eastern Belorussia, the abundance of land and limited incentives for commercial arable farming shifted the attention of tenant farmers towards animal husbandry and to the immense resources of rivers or lakes for fish and forests for honey [188]. There were also illegal activities, which often involved trespassing on seignorial property rights or monopolies. In petty trading or exploiting seignorial forests and properties, the border line between legal and illegal pursuits could be very thin, given seignorial trading monopolies or control of open resources [125]. Finally, under the conditions of a high land-to-labour ratio, as in many regions of Eastern Europe, arable income computed from the documented acreages of farms may underestimate production levels, as tenants for instance in Hungary, the Polish Commonwealth or Russia may have enjoyed easy access to considerable land reserves [153, 179, 201, 203].

The picture is incomplete without discussing dues and rents. The occurrence of high labour rents usually coincided with relatively limited rents in cash and kind [60, 119]. The customary nature of rents helped to reduce their real value due to inflation. Between 1375 and 1500, for instance, the grain value of rents in 41 Brandenburg villages fell by nearly 20 per cent. The value of rents in kind fell by 24 per cent between 1316 and 1480 [113, 116]. In Mazovia, cash rents increased from 31 *grosz* per hide before 1500 (average for Poland 24 *grosz*) to 56 *grosz* in 1564 while grain rents remained constant. In the fifteenth century, the commutation of labour services demanded an extra 33 *grosz* per hide. Taxes were about 12 to 17 *grosz* annually after 1550 for holdings comprising half a hide. This growth was offset by the greater income derived from higher grain prices [166, 201]. Simultaneous to the increase of labour rents in the district of Sandomierz in Poland, the average grain rent per full tenant farm holding decreased strongly by 15 per cent from c.290 kg of grain to c.250 kg between 1565 and 1600. Cash rents increased nominally by 75 per cent, but their real value (measured against the price inflation of rye in the region) significantly declined and finally was only a quarter of the original 1565 level. Around 1600, half and full holdings paid about 16.5 per cent of gross output in seignorial rent, while the range was between 14 and 33 per cent in Mazovia (including tithe; Table 5.4) [181]. For regions of eighteenth-century Little Poland, the total rent burden is estimated at between 22 and 30 per cent of farm income [165].

In Hungary, the value of cash rents declined at least by half between 1550 and 1650, yet the relatively high rents in kind were an additional burden [155, 159]. At the end of the sixteenth century, Livonian full holdings probably required 15.5 per cent of gross output (13 of 84 hl) for grain rents [95]. In the estate of Stavenow in Brandenburg, 1560 rent levels equalled 23.5 per cent of a tenant farm's grain output. In the eighteenth century, the value of taxes and rents as a proportion of the income of a full tenant farm decreased from 50 per cent before 1750 to 36 per cent in the period 1766–1805 [116]. For an Uckermark tenant farm, expenses for rents and taxes represented a quarter of gross income in 1723 [106]. In Boitzenburg, a farmer paid 25.7 per cent of his gross income in taxes and between 13.3 and 26.1 per cent in seignorial rent in 1766 [118].

Tax and rent levels of 16 per cent of gross income, as estimated for the rural holdings of townsmen in eighteenth-century Bohemia, appear very low in this context [78]. Another estimate for a Bohemian grain farmer (Table 5.5, example 7) finds rents and taxes at 30 per cent of gross income, of which taxes made up the major share. Production expenses were about 40 per cent of gross income. Monetary income net of all expenses and consumption was 1.3 per cent of gross income from grain sales. Production costs were estimated at 43 per cent of gross harvest on average [77]. These overall levels of 20 to 40 per cent for rents and taxes can be confirmed for other regions, such as for full farmholdings in Zealand (less than 20 per cent for tithe, rents and taxes) in c.1780 [88] or Poland (about 30 per cent for rents and taxes for a tenant farm) in the Poznán area in 1803 [182].

The eighteenth century was marked by significant changes in the rent structure in Russia. Until 1750, rents consumed about 20 per cent and taxes about 12 per cent of the gross output of tenant farms on average. Strong rent increases occurred afterwards, partly offset by a 2.5-fold rise in prices and a real decline in taxation levels. In real terms, total rent and *corvée* levels approximately doubled between 1750 and 1800. A survey for several provinces finds a gross income growth per rural household of between 40 and 70 per cent from c.1750 to 1850, but quitrents measured in silver roubles more than doubled in extreme cases. On the other hand, rents actually declined in some regions over the same period [210, 217, 222].

The overall rent structure must be considered when evaluating the actual effects of labour rents on tenant income and living standards. Cash rents were often lower in villages with labour rents than in those without. As the Polish examples quoted above illustrate, the increase in labour rents was compensated for by a significant decrease in the real value of all other feudal rents around 1600 [181]. The growth of the demesne economy in Denmark in the seventeenth and eighteenth centuries led to a substantial increase in labour rents, but at the same time this meant that rents in cash and kind stagnated. During the late eighteenth century, rents in cash and kind per hectare of farm land were 50 per cent lower for farms with labour rents than for tenants without in the East Prussian district of Ostróda. In another district, tenant farms with labour services of more than 250 days per year did not have to pay any rents in cash and kind and the lord compensated them for a part of the labour services [60]. In the west of Brandenburg, where demesne lordship did not fully develop, tenant burdens per hide were higher than in the rest of the Electorate, save for the district of extreme demesne lordship [111].

Rents usually equated a third of the gross income of Prussian farmers on princely estates and on noble estates without or with only limited labour rents. With high labour rents of more than 250 days per year, the total burden increased to 46 to 73 per cent of gross income, depending on the size of the holding [60]. Tenant farmers in eighteenth-century Schleswig-Holstein experienced a negative income effect from labour rents, though total burdens per hectare of farmland on demesne estates were as high for farms without labour rents in the less manorialised West (5.48 vs 5.53 *reichstaler* in 1766). In the west the main burden was cash rents, while on demesne estates it was labour rents. Lower output on farms with labour rents represented the major difference between the two, so that total rents consumed only 24 per cent of gross farm income in the West and 49 in the East [148]. Despite these burdens and unlike so many eighteenth-century travel reports of 'learned' visitors eager to construct a negative image of Eastern Europe [53], a Holstein account of 1740 concluded that all the serf farms in a specific area were 'in extraordinary good shape' [88, 112].

The literature generally assumes that overall levies were higher in areas of demesne lordship than in Western Europe, mainly because of labour rents. However, between 1500 and 1800 rent and tax burdens increased dramatically in the West. A recent survey showed that the rent–wage ratio (value of land rents to wages) in England, the Île-de-France and the Netherlands grew threefold in relation to a rural labourer's wages between 1500 and 1800 [61]. According to one of the few comparisons between Western and Eastern European regions, the gross monetary equivalent of all rents per hectare of farmland was actually considerably higher in western and central France, Belgium and the Netherlands than in the areas of strictest serfdom (Holstein, Mecklenburg and Pomerania) in the eighteenth century. However, income per hectare of farmland was considerably higher in the West. On average, total burdens ranged between 30 (lowest) and 50 (highest) per cent of gross income. The latter value was typical for regions with high labour rents. Based on rye prices between 1781 and 1790, the net income of tenant farmers varied between the equivalent of 300 kg per hectare of land in Flanders as a maximum and 100 kg in Eastern Poland as a minimum. However, average farm size was usually bigger in most regions of East-Central and Eastern Europe than in the West, which would make up for some of this difference on the level of total farm income [60].

The ability of tenant farmers to acquire considerable property over their life further questions the idea of an overall stagnation of rural living standards under demesne lordship. In the first third of the seventeenth century, the gross household wealth of tenant farmers in three villages of the Brandenburg estate of Wilsnack amounted to 254 to 606 *gulden* (between 131 and 222 *gulden* net of debts). The monetary equivalent of the property of smallholders was between 73 and 163 *gulden* or 36 to 96 *gulden* net of debt [135]. In the Uckermark, tenant farms were wealthy enough to buy properties in nearby towns around 1600, or acquired seignorial rights after 1650 when demesne lords were desperate to raise cash [106]. Data from the Brandenburg district of Ruppin reflect the beneficial impact of the Berlin market for increasing tenant wealth after 1770. According to post-mortem inventories, household wealth ranged between 200 and 400 *taler* even without the value of the farm buildings and the land. In 1788, Christoph Schönholz's property in Wustrau was valued at 780 *taler*, of which 60 per cent was in cash. The widow of Johann Christian Kriedt, the innkeeper of Manker, left nearly 3500 *taler* (the value of house and land made up 2200 *taler*) [121]. In the Brandenburg Uckermark – associated with personal serfdom, weak property rights and labour rents – personal wealth of between 500 and 700 *reichstaler* was regarded as normal in villages on the estate of Boitzenburg in the late 1700s [118, 120]. When Joachim Müller applied for the lease of a free tenant farm in 1783, he dispensed over 250 *reichstaler* in cash, enough to pay at once for equipment and inventory. A widow named Schultz held 1588 *reichstaler* in cash. Martin Krumrey and his wife in Bertikow bought lordship rights over the village of Bertikow for 4600 *reichstaler* in 1743, on top of running a number of tenant farms totalling more than 200 hectares. The value of their freehold property was 6400 *reichstaler* (approximately 125 kg of silver). Peter Zimmermann was tenant of a large subject holding before he leased a demesne farm in 1727 for a rent of 864 *reichstaler* per year and paid a deposit of 600 *reichstaler* in cash. With the help of sons and sons-in-law, he leased two further demesne farms and he retired in 1745 by buying a noble estate for 10 000 *reichstaler* [106]. To compare, taking Berlin prices 1766–1805, 10 *reichstaler* would have bought 275–310 kg of rye on average [116]; the daily wages of building workers were 11.5 grams of silver in London and 4.3 grams in Augsburg in the period 1750–99.

The verdicts of eighteenth-century demesne administrations stress that tenants ran sound businesses and were debt free, that their income had improved and that they tended their fields and buildings eagerly and well. Profiting from market demand, many farming villages around Berlin were described as inhabited by wealthy farmers and demesne lords, and their administrators showed themselves to be increasingly concerned about the rising self-confidence of wealthier tenants [108, 130]. Debts and financial accounts show that villagers often made transactions with considerable sums of money [116]. Villagers' wealth was not necessarily based on the ownership of land. Christian Friedrich Kemnitz, a day labourer in the Brandenburg village of Wustrau, left 100 *taler* in cash and a total estate worth 157 *taler* in 1798 [121]. There was a marked contrast between tenant households on seignorial estates in the *chernozem* region and villages in the Russian centre and north, such as on the estate of Baki, where they paid quitrent and added to household income by successfully diversifying activities into forestry, trade, handicraft and proto-industries [210, 221]. With yields of 1 : 10 in slash-and-burn agricultural activities, there was also an agricultural basis. Such evidence undermines the traditional picture of a 'wretched' Russian peasantry in 'dismal condition' [27], often taken to be synonymous for the situation in Eastern Europe as a whole [210, 212, 214, 215, 220, 221]. Intensive proto-industrialisation could help increase the living standards of cottagers and smallholders in particular regions. The well-known rich proto-industrial textile entrepreneurs of the Russian Sheremetev estates, often referred to in the literature, were serfs. Some succeeded in redeeming themselves from their lord, involving fees of up to tens of thousands of roubles [70, 212].

Part of the tradition of the victimisation of villagers in Eastern Europe since the eighteenth century is that they were generally described as living in oppression and precarious economic circumstances, that they were all 'tormented and without property' [112]. Data taken from empirical research since 1945 make obvious the serious problems with generalisations depicting Eastern European villagers as trapped in a Malthusian world between low productivity and high rent pressure so that they could hardly earn a living. A more accurate picture would stress successful tenant market participation and the progress of commercialisation. To overcome traditional images completely, systematic comparative studies on rural living standards considering all parts of Europe need to be carried out [15].

[iv]   Rural Social Structure

According to conventional approaches, demesne lordship did not only cause economic 'backwardness' in the tenant economy, but also prevented cultural and social progress and helped to maintain a traditional 'peasant' society. 'Modern' economic and social relationships, such as the spread of a rural proletariat and wage labour, could not really be established prior to the abolition of the demesne system. Therefore, social differentiation was regarded as less pronounced than in Central or Western Europe, a lack of social stratification that is often taken to characterise traditional 'peasant' societies. Studies assumed that lords were eager to conserve the traditional social order and to maintain their dominance of full-holding farms because of the labour requirements of the demesne economy [96, 118].

Contemporary sources from the area differentiate various groups of tenant farmers and separate them from smallholders, cottagers and other landless villagers. These farmers (German *Bauer*, Czech *sedlák*, Polish *kmieć*, Hungarian *jobbágy*) either had what was considered a full farm holding (usually in the range of 20–40 hectares, 45–100 acres), eligible for full labour rents, or owned only parts of a fullholding (half a holding or more). Those owning a quarter holding were usually not considered to be proper farmers (German *Kossät*, [*Erb-*]*Gärtner*, Czech *chalupník*, Polish *zagrodnik*, Hungarian *negyedtelkes jobbágy*). Finally there were smallholders, cottagers or crofters (German *Gärtner*, *Häusler*, Czech *zahrádník/domkař*, Polish *chałupnik*; *inquilinus* is the Latin term used in Hungary), who held only a small plot of land or just a building with a garden, or were completely landless. Among the latter were servants, but also lodgers living alone or with their families on farms and smallholdings (German *Inwohner*, *Hausgenosse*, Czech *podruh*, Polish *komornik*; *subinquilinus* is the Latin term used in Hungary). Rural societies in demesne lordship were thus highly stratified in terms of landed property [28, 34, 37, 70].

The traditional image of Eastern European social structure rests on the usually substantial size and alleged social and economic dominance of full tenant holdings, which one could describe as large yeomen farms and which were typical in villages of Eastern Germany, Hungary, Bohemia, Moravia or the Baltic. Many of these farms were at the threshold of what is regarded as a 'capitalist' farm

124

in England in the seventeenth and eighteenth centuries (100 acres and more). Representative examples would be Brandenburg dairy farmers in the late eighteenth century (60 hectares or 150 acres) [120], or Mecklenburg and Pomeranian hereditary village headmen (four to six hides of land or more than 120 hectares). In the late sixteenth century, such farms kept between 10 and 20 horses and up to 25 head of cattle [128]. Around 1600, farmers in Eastern Pomerania or in the Vistula Fens held 60 hectares of land, 15–20 horses and a substantial number of cattle [178]. On the estate of Boitzenburg in the Brandenburg Uckermark in 1800, the average size of arable land of the 189 tenant farmholdings in 11 villages was 37.8 hectares. In 1625, the average farm in the area held four horses and seven oxen; inventories of the mid-eighteenth century show three to four horses or four to seven oxen per farmstead [118]. For such vast farms we really need not shy away from comparison with large commercial farms in England or the *fermiers* of the Île-de-France.

Fullholdings were large, but not necessarily as large as these examples. In a late seventeenth-century survey of 3313 tenant holdings in 1103 villages of Swedish Pomerania, full tenant farms had on average 18 hectares of land and employed 2.3 servants [144]. Data from a tax survey in Mecklenburg-Schwerin in 1703 indicate farm size by the quantity of arable seed. About 70 per cent of the farms needed seed of between 26 and 75 *scheffel* (roughly between 6 and 19 hectares); only slightly more than 20 per cent were smaller than 25 *scheffel* (approximately 5 hectares). The group with seed of more than 75 *scheffel* can be regarded as substantial fullholders and represented about 25 per cent of all farmsteads. They kept livestock of 6 to 8 horses and 8.6 to 15.7 cattle on average [143]. In eighteenth-century Holstein, fullholdings were large enough to provide not only the necessary draught and manpower to work their 20–50 hectares, but also to be able to supply two additional draught teams with four horses each and up to five workers for the demesne farms. Labour rent burdens demanded that the number of horses on such farms would be high (seven to fourteen), yet the number of cattle was relatively low (four to six) [112, 148].

An estimate for East Prussia sets average tenant farm size at 31.6 hectares (just below 80 acres). Such farms held between four and six horses and two to four oxen as draught animals in the first half of the eighteenth century [60]. According to probate inventories in the Brandenburg estate of Wilsnack, full farms held between

7 and 9.5 horses on average in 1610–30, and smallholders 3.5 horses [135]. Tenant farms in Stavenow kept five work horses and five cattle on average in 1721–71 [116]. Though the average holding size of full farmsteads in the agricultural heartland of central Bohemia slightly declined from 23 hectares to 21.3 hectares between 1654 and the 1720s, average number of livestock increased. In the estate of Poděbrady, such farms held 1.9 head of draught animals on average after the Thirty Years' War (probably a depressed figure because of the impact of the war); it increased to 3.1 horses and 1.3 oxen as well as 3.9 cows until the 1720s [70].

Polish studies indentify a long-term decrease in the size of the average tenant holding between the sixteenth and eighteenth centuries. Most farms nevertheless maintained a size that would continuously support a livelihood [28, 160, 170]. The analysis of holding size does not give the full picture, however. Villagers tended to lease additional land (such as from desertions or unused areas), which did not count towards their regular tenure. For example, on one Belorussian estate tenants held 26 to 28 hectares between 1650 and 1750, but only half of this area actually belonged to the farmsteads [188, 201, 204]. In addition, there were quite pronounced regional differences in tenant landholding structure, so that we actually observe different and partly contradictory trends among the various parts of the commonwealth [166, 179]. Full holdings and a stratum of rich tenant farmers did not completely disappear anywhere. In the sixteenth century, the average livestock was five to six cattle, four to five horses and two oxen [170, 201, 203]. In 150 villages of the Gniezno episcopal property, farmers held six horses on average in 1544, a number that decreased until the 1650s. Oxen were kept instead, so the total count of draught animals was still four on average [189]. Tenant farmers in seventeenth-century Little Poland and eighteenth-century Great Poland held three to four oxen and two horses [182, 191].

A similar trend of a growing share of smaller farmsteads and smallholdings was observed in late sixteenth- and early seventeenth-century Livonia and may have been due to labour and capital scarcity. It seems that even fullholdings did not work the whole area of land available to them [95]. In the seventeenth century, a full farmholding was defined as comprising 18 hectares of arable land. Such a tenant farm would usually keep two and maybe up to four plough teams, and two to three male and female servants. Smaller farms would hold one or two draught teams on average [94, 95, 97]. A typical Russian tenant farm on a *barshchina* estate was also rather small by comparison (about 22 acres) and held two or three working horses [214].

In contrast to the traditional interest in large-scale tenant farms, new research shows that social and property differentiation in East-Central and Eastern Europe was not generally less pronounced than in the West. In certain areas, groups of smallholders and the landless actually dominated. They can be observed in significant numbers as early as the later Middle Ages [69] and their share among rural households increased strongly almost everywhere between 1500 and 1800 [28, 34, 70, 72, 95, 162]. The re-orientation of the system towards wage labour after 1700, as well as a late wave of expropriations, contributed significantly to the further growth of smallholders and the landless, for instance in Mecklenburg. It is one of the striking features of the duchy that in noble demesne estates entire villages consisted of agricultural labourers and smallholders only, once all the farms were expropriated [40]. Table 5.6 summarises the significance of rural social groups below the level of full or half holdings in the area (with the exception of Russia) for the eighteenth century.

Table 5.6 The proportion of smallholdings and the landless in selected territories of East-Central and Eastern Europe, c.1700–1800 (in % of all rural households)

Territory	Share of smallholdings/cottagers
Bohemia	57
Brandenburg	66*
Denmark	40
Eastern Pomerania	60*
East Prussia	57*
Great Poland	77
Little Poland	60–84
Livonia	25–30
Mecklenburg	73
Silesia	76
Upper Lusatia	71
Western Pomerania	22

Note: *Including lodgers.
Sources: [14, 34, 56, 70, 103, 143, 144, 165, 170, 171].

Early modern social and cultural change and the emergence of landless and land-poor strata were thus part and parcel of rural society in regions of demesne lordship. The traditional 'peasant' structure was not preserved. By contrast, the majority of the rural population was formed by groups with little or no landholding, while classic tenant farmers with their full and half holdings formed a substantial minority in nearly all of the areas surveyed. Villages and lords accommodated these new groups flexibly and with a range of strategies, either by opening up common land, by leasing or selling plots of tenant land to cottagers or by partitioning demesnes as well as opening land reserves for new settlements. The socio-economic structure of villages changed totally with the continuous growth of these groups, who could not rely on an independent agricultural livelihood [72]. This pronounced social differentiation also led to the fact that, like in the West, rural communities did not form socially coherent entities. On the contrary, they were highly stratified and had to cope with a diversity of interests and a range of inner conflicts [81, 85, 142, 214, 220]. Smallholders and cottagers faced different challenges and possibly followed other strategies within communal politics and vis-à-vis demesne lords than did fullholders or privileged groups of tenants such as village headmen. The burdens of demesne lordship could also weigh differently for the individual social groups. Although it seems that fullholdings bore the brunt of full labour rents, burdens were relatively higher for owners of smaller properties or cottagers. Certain negative influences of demesne lordship may have been stronger for the poor [210].

[v]   Conclusions

This chapter has surveyed some of the empirical evidence regarding the view that demesne lordship and the demesne economy represented institutions that caused long-term economic 'backwardness' for the entire East Elbian area. The system was supposed to have kept villagers' living standards and well-being at a minimum and to have shaped a market-averse, traditional peasant society. As for the long-term consequences for economic growth, a general assessment will have to wait for future comparative studies on aggregate growth before 1800. Here, doubts were raised over the traditional argument by discussing agricultural productivity and innovation within the demesne economy and by summarising the available evidence on rural living standards.

Agricultural yields varied widely and, in aggregate terms, did not reach the levels of the most advanced agricultural areas of Europe at the time. The range of grain yields, however, does not give the impression of overall stagnation and points to the necessity to differentiate. This conclusion is bolstered by studies that specifically address the adaptability of the system and the evidence for agrarian innovation. In Western European economic history, stagnationist theories of a 'Malthusian-Ricardian' pre-modern rural economy, assumed to be always on the verge of famine and a mortality crisis, have been increasingly criticised over the last few decades and have given way to a more favourable assessment of economic flexibility and dynamics in this period [8, 13]. There is a sound empirical basis to conclude that this is also justified for the early modern Eastern European economy. Quite contrary to the image of a traditional peasant society maintained by demesne lordship, extensive market participation was widespread among tenant farmers and smallholders. A possible negative impact of demesne lordship must not be ignored, but must be put into the context of other concrete factors, such as the bigger size of tenant farms compared to Western Europe or the relatively low burden of cash and product rents or taxes. Finally, future analysis of the economic development of early modern Eastern Europe also needs to pay more attention to the widespread development of proto-industrialisation in the area.

In size and equipment, Eastern European full tenant holdings can easily be compared to large commercial Western European tenant and yeomen farms. They displayed the same characteristics of a commercial orientation and a combination of family and wage labour from servants and agricultural workers. The survey of social structure shows that the existence of a landless population in the early modern period was not limited to Western European societies, but also occurred in East-Central and Eastern Europe. Social and property differentiation progressed over the early modern period and this does not lend support to the conventional hypothesis that demesne lords actively pursued a policy of preserving a traditional peasant society; rather, they adapted flexibly to social change, as did village communities.

6 Towards a New Assessment

This book started with the traditional description of rural societies in early modern East-Central Europe, according to which they experienced a significant rise in the power of landlords. This is claimed to have led to a stricter form of the seignorial system (demesne lordship) and the growth of a commercial demesne economy. It was assumed to be accompanied by the deterioration of village autonomy and an erosion in the legal and economic status of villagers and their property rights. These were the two pillars – strong lords and weak, bonded villagers – regarded as characteristic of early modern Eastern European rural societies. The previous interpretation put these at the heart of the idea of a fundamental East–West divide in early modern rural Europe, synonymous with the idea of a liberal and modernising West and a backward East. From the 1960s onwards, research gradually began to question this meta-narrative.

Even today, surveys claim a general lack of freedom and bondage of villagers in early modern Europe east of the river Elbe. The preceding chapters have strongly disagreed with this assertion. According to the argument developed in this book, the 'dualism' in agrarian structure and the notion of a 'second serfdom' lasting unchanged for 300 years can no longer be maintained as a general interpretation. The original assessment may have been a useful conception for certain macro-level accounts of early modern European development, but the results of empirical research over the last 25 years have all but eroded its basis. East-Central and Eastern Europe did not represent a compact entity of second serfdom. Rather, rural social structures were significantly differentiated by time and place. The comparative view adopted in this volume helps to overcome earlier approaches and explanations based on the analysis of individual territories and regions. It avoids the chronic mistake in much of the literature before the 1990s that, by concentrating only on developments in a particular territory or country, either offered explanations specific to that case or emphasised a particular characteristic to justify results that were not in line with the existing oversimplified generalisations, but never challenged the latter in the first place.

More specific to the research on which this book has focused, the concept of demesne lordship was used in different ways over the twentieth century. Recent criticism has concentrated on uniformity of the associated patterns. Although it represents a useful tool for analysing seignorial structures in East-Elbian Europe, particularly for approaches concentrating on the legal and political aspects, recent research suggests the existence of many variations in the relationship between villagers and lords. Serfdom among the rural population could be a consequence of an extreme variant of demesne lordship, but remained a limited phenomenon both regionally and chronologically. Its actual occurrence must be seen as the results of particular developments that cannot be generalised over the whole area. It is therefore important to differentiate between the potential powers of lords and actual practices. Studies concentrating on the latter, which give more room to the perspective of villagers, reveal important revisions of the original picture. There was a dominant tendency to maintain hereditary tenure as well as secure property rights and significant functions of village communities and their institutions. Villagers enjoyed considerable autonomy with regard to their economic and social affairs. They were actively involved in shaping the everyday local and estate context. Seignorial pressure met with accommodation, but also resistance and insubordination. Labour rents were negotiated or settled by extensive court battles rather than simply imposed; seventeenth- and eighteenth-century mobility restrictions oscillated between strict imposition, liberal practices (in exchange for fees) and widespread undermining by migration and thousands of fugitives. Recent detailed research does not confirm the systematic interference of lords in the independent economic decisions of villagers' households or their family and inheritance strategies.

How do these findings relate to different conclusions of other detailed case studies focusing in the same manner on social practices and the everyday consequences of demesne lordship? As paradoxical as it may seem, the negative effects of certain manifestations of demesne lordship that these studies reveal do not contradict the arguments developed here. Serfdom, where it existed, could have extremely drastic consequences. Demesne lordship could be oppressive and lords did misuse their powers, seized from the late medieval and early modern state. In order to understand and evaluate these specific cases in their relation to the level of independence and autonomy described before, it is important to bear in mind that neither subjects nor serfs were helpless victims. They turned to the authorities, to insubordination or to open protest to oppose these tendencies, and generally did so not entirely unsuccessfully, although they were more successful in some regions and periods than in others. Even when they failed, they nevertheless contributed to shaping the concrete relationship on the local level, and this needs to be analysed within its context through a detailed case study. Villagers also formed an integral part in the execution of seignorial (or state) power. This understanding of 'power as social practice' [39, 54] accounts for the fact that the outcome varied over time and place. We must expect to find the complete spectrum from oppression to local and regional societies in which tenant farmers, smallholders and cottagers thrived relatively unaffected by rent levels or the *de iure* powers of their lords. As Steven Hoch put it in his detailed reconstruction of life on a Russian *barshchina* estate: 'Serfdom was not a system, but a widely varying set of practices' [214]. In the majority of regions analysed here serfdom did not exist; in many, seignorial practices were much looser. The overall effects were far from general suppression and backwardness, economically, socially or culturally.

Various theories have been proposed to explain the rise of the commercial demesne economy during the early modern period. As much as explanations based on grain exports would fit macro theories of a European dualism and the peripheralisation of Eastern Europe within a European division of labour, in most cases they do not match the chronology and type of exports, nor the significance of domestic factors. Approaches referring to long-term continuity since the later Middle Ages also need careful evaluation, as empirical research over the last two decades has pointed out major discontinuities that undermine the 'constitutional' determinism suggested by older theories. Explanations ignoring long-term developments altogether, such as those linking demesne lordship to the consequences of the Thirty Years' War or the crisis of the seventeenth century, cannot be maintained if one considers a comparative approach. Thus, the most promising approach seems to be a long-term perspective including the later Middle Ages, concentrating on specific aspects of demesne development in each case rather than proposing general continuity as the central factor.

With the exception of Russia, the first surge of the commercial demesne economy occurred during the sixteenth century. Despite this uniformity, the trend was very weak in many regions, or remained marginal and short-lived. Strong discontinuities in further growth can be observed, such as in Hungary or the Baltic regions, and the final density of demesne activities and their importance for seignorial income varied enormously between regions and estates, even within the same territory. Similar observations can be made with reference to the use of labour rents. Demesne farms usually continued to employ servants and day labourers as well as exploiting labour rents. Attempts to increase labour rents in areas of an extension of demesnes during the seventeenth and eighteenth centuries met structural obstacles (such as an insufficient number of operating tenant farms until 1700) or the growing resistance of a self-confident rural population, ready to take on court battles with their lords. Once beyond a threshold of two or three days per week per full tenant farm, labour rents formed the strongest consequence of demesne lordship. By contrast, other rents usually remained limited or even declined in value over time.

Since the 1960s, empirical studies have shown a highly differentiated picture of rural economic development in early modern East-Central and Eastern Europe, which has cast doubt on the image of a structural economic backwardness. Rural societies in East-Central and Eastern Europe were characterised by the successful market participation of demesne and tenant farms and smallholdings, innovations and a differentiated social structure, with a strong growth of cottagers and the landless since the sixteenth century. The image of a market-averse, traditional 'peasant' economy and society that are thought to have been preserved by demesne lordship does not correspond to the results emerging from empirical research on the tenant economy and the development of the rural social structure. Though an aggregate comparison in terms of economic development awaits assessment, the conclusion seems justified that there was no overall stagnation in early modern East-Central and Eastern Europe in economic and social respects. Demesne lordship was not a progressive institutional organisation, but it was varied and flexible enough to accommodate, adapt to and integrate agrarian innovation, socio-structural change, proto-industrial development and commercialisation. Malthusian-Ricardian readings of early modern Western European rural societies have come under pressure since the early 1980s; neither should they be maintained for Eastern Europe.

Current research on rural societies in early modern East-Central and Eastern Europe still uses the concept of demesne lordship, but, generally speaking, this is no longer understood to represent a uniform agrarian system within a European dualism. At the same time, studies based on this new understanding do not neglect differences between East and West. To begin with, labour rents were much rarer in the West or did not occur at all, and extreme burdens of three or more days per week can only be observed in particular areas of Eastern Europe. A similar observation can be made for direct management of demesne operations. Far from existing everywhere in East Elbia, in many regions the pattern of cultivation was much more widespread than in the West. Finally, there was pressure on the social and legal status of the rural population, such as mobility restrictions, which could be different from the experience of lordship and power in the West. Microhistorical case studies will continue assessing these particular characteristics from a comparative viewpoint and may confirm strong variation on the local level. However, we could also start by making similarities across all of Europe rather than structural divisions the default hypothesis. Then, the idea of one particular successful path of modernisation (in the West, or some of it) and of lagging behind (in the East) would have to be abandoned for good. Why should we maintain blunt modernisation theories in this respect, when they have been all but abandoned in all other fields of historical research? In its turn, comparative European rural history concentrating on asymmetric power relations that, in one form or another, existed all over early modern Europe will render the concept of demesne lordship obsolete.

Nowadays, the concept of demesne lordship is used with caution and encompasses a wide range of possible manifestations, which range from milder forms resembling rent-based seignorial systems of the ancien régime in other parts of Europe to the strictest forms of subjection and even serfdom. A new view, stressing the specific mechanisms that could shape the system on the estate and local level, does not overlook possible systematic differences between East and West, but understands these as a question of degree and does not reduce them to a fundamental divide on an abstract constitutional level. As a result, the idea of a 'second serfdom' all over East-Central and Eastern Europe in the early modern period and of a European 'agrarian dualism' can no longer be maintained. To buttress this important set of revisions, future empirical research on early modern societies and economies of demesne lordship has to focus on questions such as land and labour productivity, and more generally on standards of living from a comparative perspective, as well as establishing a firm picture of welfare in rural societies.

While these two notions of a macro-historical interpretation (backwardness and dualism) can be regarded as outdated in many respects, another interpretation of the dualism concept is currently reappearing with a vengeance among studies emphasising the commercial lead of the European North-West over the rest. To counter such tendencies, often the result of a certain negligence towards other approaches and research elsewhere, one cannot help but point at results already available, which show that there was no overall rural stagnation and present demesne and tenant economic activities as flexible, changing over time and market related. Despite the possible negative consequences of demesne lordship, tenant households were able to follow independent decisions and strategies. The previously dominant image of a 'traditional peasantry' in this area, oppressed and always at the margins of existence, should no longer be maintained. To assess early modern European economic development from a comparative perspective acknowledging these revisions will require historians of (North-) Western Europe also to abandon the traditional images.

Bibliography

General and Comparative

[1]   T. Aston and C. H. E. Philpin (eds), *The Brenner debate. Agrarian class structure and economic development in pre-industrial Europe* (Cambridge, 1988).

[2]   J. Blum, 'The rise of serfdom in Eastern Europe', *American Historical Review* 62 (1957), 807–36.

[3]   M. Bush (ed.), *Serfdom and slavery. Studies in legal bondage* (London, 1996).

[4]   M. Bush, 'Serfdom in medieval and modern Europe: a comparison', in M. Bush (ed.), *Serfdom and slavery. Studies in legal bondage* (London, 1996), 199–224.

[5]   M. Cerman, 'Venkovské společnosti a agrárně-dějepisecké tvoření modelů v nové perspektivě. Srovnávací analýza středo- a východo-evropských agrárních struktur od 14. do 17. století', *Časopis Matice moravské* 120, 2 (2001), 337–95.

[6]   M. Cerman, 'Agrardualismus in Europa? Geschichtsschreibung über Gutsherrschaft und ländliche Gesellschaften in Mittel- und Osteuropa', *Jahrbuch für Geschichte des ländlichen Raumes* 1 (2004), 12–29.

[7]   M. Cerman, 'Social structure and land markets in late medieval Central and East-Central Europe', *Continuity and Change* 23, 1 (2008), 55–100.

[8]   M. Cerman, 'Rural economy and society', in P. Wilson (ed.), *A companion to eighteenth-century Europe* (Oxford, 2008), 47–65.

[9]   M. Cerman, 'Open fields, tenurial rights and the development of land markets in medieval East-Central Europe', in G. Béaur, J.-M. Chevet, M.-T. Perez-Picazo and P. Schofield (eds), *Property rights, land market and economic growth in Europe* (Turnhout, in print).

[10] M. Cerman, 'Constrained labour in early-modern rural East-Central and Eastern Europe: regional variation and its causes', in A. Stanziani (ed.), *Labour constraints in Europe and Asia* (New York/Leiden, In Print).

[11] D. Chirot (ed.), *The origins of backwardness in Eastern Europe. Economics and politics from the Middle Ages until the early twentieth century* (Cambridge, 1989).

[12] E. Domar, 'The causes of slavery and serfdom: a hypothesis', *Journal of Economic History* 30 (1970), 18–32.

[13] G. Grantham, 'Contra Ricardo: on the macroeconomics of pre-industrial economies', *European Review of Economic History* 3 (1999), 199–232.

Bibliography

[14]   P. Gunst and T. Hoffmann (eds), *Large estates and small holdings in the Middle Ages and modern times* (Budapest, 1982).

[15]   W. W. Hagen, 'European yeomanries: a non-immiseration model of agrarian social history, 1350–1800', *Agricultural History Review*, 59 (1991), 259–65.

[16]   H. Harnisch, 'Die Gutsherrschaft. Forschungsgeschichte, Entwicklungszusammenhänge und Strukturelemente', *Jahrbuch für Geschichte des Feudalismus* 9 (1985), 189–240.

[17]   H. Harnisch, 'Probleme einer Periodisierung und regionalen Typisierung der Gutsherrschaft im mitteleuropäischen Raum', *Jahrbuch für Geschichte des Feudalismus* 10 (1986), 251–74.

[18]   G. Heitz, 'Agrarischer Dualismus, Eigentumsverhältnisse, Preußischer Weg', in *Studia historica in honorem Hans Kruus* (Talinn, 1971), 303–14.

[19]   G. Heitz, 'Wirtschafts- und sozialgeschichtliche Aspekte der "zweiten Leibeigenschaft"', in V. Zimányi (ed.), *Studien zur deutschen und ungarischen Wirtschaftsentwicklung (16.–20. Jh.)* (Budapest, 1985), 43–51.

[20]   M. Hroch and J. Petráň, *17. století – krize feudální společnosti?* (Prague, 1976).

[21]   P. Janssens and B. Yun Casalilla (eds), *European aristocracies and colonial elites. Patrimonial management strategies and economic development, 15th–18th centuries* (Aldershot, 2005).

[22]   H. Kaak, *Die Gutsherrschaft. Theoriegeschichtliche Untersuchungen zum Agrarwesen im ostelbischen Raum* (Berlin, 1991).

[23]   H. Kaak and M. Schattkowsky (eds), *Herrschaft. Machtentfaltung über adligen und fürstlichen Grundbesitz in der Frühen Neuzeit* (Cologne, 2003).

[24]   A. Kahan, 'Notes on serfdom in Western and Eastern Europe', *Journal of Economic History* 33, 1 (1973), 86–99.

[25]   J. Klußmann (ed.), *Leibeigenschaft. Bäuerliche Unfreiheit in der frühen Neuzeit* (Cologne, 2003).

[26]   G. F. Knapp, *Die Bauernbefreiung und der Ursprung der Landarbeiter in den älteren Teilen Preußens*. 2 vols (Leipzig, 1887).

[27]   P. Kolchin, *Unfree labor. American slavery and Russian serfdom* (Cambridge, MA, 1987).

[28]   P. Kriedte, *Peasants, landlords and merchant capitalists* (Leamington Spa, 1983).

[29]   W. Kula, *An economic theory of the feudal system. Towards a model of the Polish economy, 1500-1800* (London, 1976).

[30]   F. Lütge, 'Grundherrschaft und Gutsherrschaft', *Handwörterbuch der Sozialwissenschaften*. Vol. 4 (Tübingen, 1965), 682–8.

[31]   A. Mączak, H. Samsonowicz and P. Burke (eds), *East-Central Europe in transition. From the fourteenth to the seventeenth century* (Cambridge, 1985).

[32]   M. Małowist, 'Die Getreidehandelspolitik des Adels in den Ostseeländern', *Hansische Geschichtsblätter* 75 (1957), 29–47.

[33]   M. Małowist, 'The economic and social development of the Baltic countries from the fifteenth to the seventeenth centuries', *Economic History Review* 12 (1959), 177–89.

[34]   E. Melton, 'Gutsherrschaft in East Elbian Germany and in Livonia, 1500–1800: a critique of the model', *Central European History* 21 (1988), 315–49.

Bibliography

[35] R. Millward, 'An economic analysis of the organization of serfdom in Eastern Europe', *Journal of Economic History* 42 (1982), 513–48.

[36] M. North, 'Die Entstehung der Gutswirtschaft im südlichen Ostseeraum', *Zeitschrift für historische Forschung* 26, 1 (1999), 43–59.

[37] J. Peters, 'Ostelbische Landarmut. Sozialökonomisches über landlose und landarme Agrarproduzenten im Spätfeudalismus', *Jahrbuch für Wirtschaftsgeschichte* 3 (1967), 255–302.

[38] J. Peters, 'Eigensinn und Widerstand im Alltag. Abwehrverhalten ostelbischer Bauern unter Refeudalisierungsdruck', *Jahrbuch für Wirtschaftsgeschichte* 2 (1991), 85–103.

[39] J. Peters, 'Gutsherrschaftsgeschichte in historisch-anthropologischer Perspektive', in J. Peters (ed.), *Gutsherrschaft als soziales Modell* (Munich, 1995), 3–21.

[40] J. Peters (ed.), *Gutsherrschaft als soziales Modell. Vergleichende Betrachtungen zur Funktionsweise frühneuzeitlicher Agrargesellschaften* (Munich, 1995).

[41] J. Peters (ed.), *Konflikt und Kontrolle in Gutsherrschaftsgesellschaften* (Göttingen, 1995).

[42] J. Peters (ed.), *Gutsherrschaftsgesellschaften im europäischen Vergleich* (Berlin, 1997).

[43] J. Peters, 'Neue Ansätze zur Erforschung der Geschichte der ländlichen Gesellschaft', in L. Enders and K. Neitmann (eds), *Brandenburgische Landesgeschichte heute* (Potsdam, 1999), 33–68.

[44] J. Peters, 'Gutsherrschaftsgeschichte und kein Ende. Versuch einer Auskunft zu aktuellen Ergebnissen und Schwierigkeiten in der Forschung', in E. Münch and R. Schattkowsky (eds), *Festschrift für Gerhard Heitz zum 75. Geburtstag* (Rostock, 2000), 53–80.

[45] C. Schmidt, *Leibeigenschaft im Ostseeraum. Versuch einer Typologie* (Cologne, 1997).

[46] T. Scott (ed.), *The peasantries of Europe* (London, 1998).

[47] H. Sundhaussen, 'Zur Wechselbeziehung zwischen frühneuzeitlichem Außenhandel und ökonomischer Rückständigkeit in Osteuropa. Eine Auseinandersetzung mit der Kolonialthese', *Geschichte und Gesellschaft* 9 (1983), 544–63.

[48] H. Sundhaussen, 'Der Wandel in der osteuropäischen Agrarverfassung während der frühen Neuzeit. Ein Beitrag zur Divergenz der Entwicklungswege von Ost- und Westeuropa', *Südost-Forschungen* 49 (1990), 15–56.

[49] J. Topolski, *Narodziny kapitalizmu w Europie XIV–XVII wieku* (Warsaw, 1965).

[50] I. Wallerstein, *The modern world system. Vols 1–2* (New York, 1976–80).

[51] P. S. Wandycz, *The price of freedom. A history of East Central Europe from the Middle Ages to the present* (London, 1993).

[52] W. Wittich, 'Gutsherrschaft', *Handwörterbuch der Staatswissenschaften*. Vol. 4 (Jena, 1905), 290–1.

[53] L. Wolff, *Inventing Eastern Europe. The map of civilization on the mind of the Enlightenment* (Stanford, 1994).

Bibliography

[54] H. Wunder, 'Das Selbstverständliche denken. Ein Vorschlag zur vergleichenden Analyse ländlicher Gesellschaften in der Frühen Neuzeit, ausgehend vom "Modell ostelbische Gutsherrschaft"', in J. Peters (ed.), *Gutsherrschaft als soziales Modell. Vergleichende Betrachtungen zur Funktionsweise frühneuzeitlicher Agrargesellschaften* (München, 1995), 23–49.

[55] L. Żytkowicz, 'Trends of agrarian economy in Poland, Bohemia and Hungary from the middle of the fifteenth to the middle of the seventeenth century', in A. Mączak, H. Samsonowicz and P. Burke (eds), *East-Central Europe in transition* (Cambridge, 1985), 59–83.

Data and Surveys

[56] W. Abel, *Geschichte der deutschen Landwirtschaft vom frühen Mittelalter bis zum 19. Jahrhundert* (Stuttgart, 1978).

[57] N. Bang and K. Korst, *Tabeller over skibsfart og varetransport gennem Øresund, 1497–1783.* 7 vols. (Copenhagen 1906–53).

[58] I. Bog (ed.), *Der Außenhandel Ostmitteleuropas 1450–1650. Die ostmitteleuropäischen Volkswirtschaften in ihren Beziehungen zu Mitteleuropa* (Cologne, 1971).

[59] E. Cieślak and C. Biernat, *History of Gdańsk* (Gdańsk, 1988).

[60] F.-W. Henning, *Dienste und Abgaben der Bauern im 18. Jahrhundert* (Stuttgart, 1969).

[61] P. Malanima, *Pre-modern European economy* (Leiden, 2009).

[62] R. Rybarski, *Handel i polityka handlowa Polski w XVI stuleciu.* 2 vols (Warsaw, 1958).

[63] B. H. Slicher van Bath, *Yield ratios, 810–1820* (Wageningen, 1963).

[64] B. H. Slicher van Bath, 'Agriculture in the vital revolution', in E. E. Rich and C. H. Wilson (eds), *The Cambridge economic history of Europe. Vol. 5. The economic organization of early modern Europe* (Cambridge, 1977), 42–132.

Regional Studies

Czech Lands

[65] J. Čechura, *Die Struktur der Grundherrschaften im mittelalterlichen Böhmen* (Stuttgart, 1994).

[66] J. Čechura, 'Die Gutswirtschaft des Adels in Böhmen in der Epoche vor der Schlacht am Weißen Berg', *Bohemia* 36 (1995), 1–18.

[67] J. Čechura, *Adelige Grundherrn als Unternehmer. Zur Struktur südböhmischer Dominien vor 1620* (Vienna, 2000).

Bibliography

[68] M. Cerman, 'Gutsherrschaft und untertäniges Gewerbe: die Herrschaften Frýdlant und Liberec in Nordböhmen', *Jahrbücher für Geschichte Osteuropas* 47, 1 (1999), 2–19.

[69] M. Cerman and R. Luft (eds), *Untertanen, Herrschaft und Staat in Böhmen und im 'Alten Reich'. Sozialgeschichtliche Perspektiven* (Munich, 2005).

[70] M. Cerman and E. Maur, 'Proměny vesnických sociálních struktur v Čechách 1650–1750', *Český časopis historický* 98 (2000), 737–74.

[71] M. Cerman and D. Štefanová, 'Institutional changes and peasant land transfer in the Czech Lands from the late Middle Ages to the eighteenth century', in R. Congost and R. Santos (eds), *Contexts of property in Europe. The social embeddedness of property rights in land in historical perspective* (Turnhout, 2011), 39–59.

[72] M. Cerman and H. Zeitlhofer (eds), *Soziale Strukturen in Böhmen. Ein regionaler Vergleich von Wirtschaft und Gesellschaft in Gutsherrschaften, 16.–19. Jahrhundert* (Vienna, 2002).

[73] J. Grulich, *Populační vývoj a životní cyklus venkovského obyvatelstva na jihu Čech v 16. až 18. století* (České Budějovice, 2008).

[74] E. Janoušek, *Historický vývoj produktivity prace v zemědělství v období pobělohorském* (Prague, 1967).

[75] J. Kočí, 'Patent o zrušení nevolnictví v českých zemích', *Československý časopis historický* 17 (1969), 69–108.

[76] A. Kostlán, 'Die Wandlungen sozialer Ordnungssysteme. Untertanen und Gutsherrschaft in Böhmen und Mähren vom 16.–18. Jahrhundert', in J. Peters (ed.), *Gutsherrschaftsgesellschaften im europäischen Vergleich* (Berlin, 1997), 113–19.

[77] J. Křivka, 'Příspěvky k dějinám poddanského hospodáření v první polovici 18. stol.', *Sborník Československé akademie zemědělských věd – Historie a musejnictví* 30 (1957), 79–94, 301–20.

[78] J. Křivka, *Výrobní a peněžní výsledky měšťanského zemědělství v 18. století v severních Čechách* (Prague, 1975).

[79] F. Matějek, *Feudalní velkostatek a poddany na Moravě s přihlédnutim k přilehlému území Slezska a Polska* (Prague, 1959).

[80] E. Maur, *Gutsherrschaft und "zweite Leibeigenschaft" in Böhmen. Studien zur Wirtschafts-, Sozial- und Bevölkerungsgeschichte (14.–18. Jahrhundert)* (Munich, 2001).

[81] S. Ogilvie, 'Communities and the "second serfdom" in early modern Bohemia', *Past and Present* 187 (2005), 69–120.

[82] J. Petráň, *Poddany lid v Čechách na prahu třicetileté války* (Prague, 1964).

[83] J. Petráň, 'Die mitteleuropäische Landwirtschaft und der Handel im 16. und am Anfang des 17. Jahrhunderts', *Historica* 18 (1973), 105–38.

[84] D. Štefanová, 'Ökonomie der Altenteiler in einer gutsherrlichen Gesellschaft, Herrschaft Frýdlant 1558–1750', in S. Lesemann and A. Lubinski (eds), *Ländliche Ökonomien* (Berlin, 2007), 251–86.

[85] D. Štefanová, *Erbschaftspraxis, Besitztransfer und Handlungsspielräume von Untertanen in der Gutsherrschaft. Die Herrschaft Frýdlant in Nordböhmen, 1558–1750* (Munich, 2009).

[86] J. Válka, *Hospodářská politika feudálního velkostatku na předbělohorské Moravě* (Brno, 1962).

Bibliography

[87]   A. Velková, *Krutá vrchnost, ubozí poddaní? Proměny venkovské rodiny a společnosti v 18. a první polovině 19. století na příkladu zapadočeského panství Šťáhlavy* (Prague, 2009).

Denmark, Finland, Sweden

[88]   P. O. Christiansen, *A manorial world. Lord, peasants and cultural distinctions on a Danish estate, 1750–1980* (Oslo, 1996).
[89]   E. Jutikkala, 'Large scale farming in Scandinavia in the seventeenth century', *Scandinavian Economic History Review* 23 (1975), 159–66.
[90]   M. Olsson, 'Peasant freedom and noble dominance. Scania in early modern times', in J. Klußmann (ed.), *Leibeigenschaft. Bäuerliche Unfreiheit in der frühen Neuzeit* (Cologne, 2003), 117–34.
[91]   M. Olsson, 'Manorial economy and corvée labour in Southern Sweden, 1650–1850', *Economic History Review* 59 (2006), 481–97.
[92]   E. L. Petersen, 'The Danish cattle trade during the sixteenth and seventeenth centuries', *Scandinavian Economic History Review* 28 (1970), 69–85.

Eastern Baltic

[93]   V. Dorošenko, 'Der ostbaltische Herrenhof des 16.–18. Jahrhunderts als "Getreidefabrik"', in A. Guarducci (ed.), *Agricoltura e trasformazione dell'ambiente secoli XIII–XVIII* (Prato, 1981).
[94]   E. Dunsdorf, *The Livonian estates of Axel Oxenstierna* (Stockholm, 1981).
[95]   J. Heyde, *Bauer, Gutshof und Königsmacht. Die estnischen Bauern in Livland unter polnischer und schwedischer Herrschaft 1561–1650* (Cologne, 2000).
[96]   J. Kahk, *Peasant and lord in the process of transition from feudalism to capitalism in the Baltics* (Tallinn, 1982).
[97]   J. Kahk, 'The regulation of peasant duties in Estonia in the 17th–19th centuries and the myth of the "good Swedish era"', in J. Selovuori (ed.), *Vaikka voissa paistais? Venäjän rooli Suomessa. Juhlakirja professori Osmo Jussilalle* (Helsinki, 1998), 462–92.
[98]   J. Kahk and E. Tarvel, *An economic history of the Baltic countries* (Stockholm, 1997).
[99]   M. Seppel, 'Die Entwicklung der livländischen Leibeigenschaft im 16. und 17. Jahrhundert', *Zeitschrift für Ostmitteleuropa-Forschung* 54 (2005), 174–93.
[100]   A. Soom, *Der Herrenhof in Estland im 17. Jahrhundert* (Lund, 1954).
[101]   A. Soom, *Der baltische Getreidehandel im 17. Jahrhundert* (Stockholm, 1961).

Germany

[102]   K. Baumgarten and U. Bentzien, *Hof und Wirtschaft der Ribnitzer Bauern. Edition und Kommentar des Kloster-Inventariums von 1620* (Berlin, 1963).

Bibliography

[103]   W. Boelcke, *Bauer und Gutsherr in der Oberlausitz. Ein Beitrag zur Wirtschafts-, Sozial- und Rechtsgeschichte der ostelbischen Gutsherrschaft* (Bautzen, 1957).

[104]   F. Carsten, *The origins of Prussia* (Oxford, 1954).

[105]   H. Dade, *Die Entstehung der mecklenburgischen Schlagwirthschaft* (Göttingen, 1891).

[106]   L. Enders, *Die Uckermark. Geschichte einer kurmärkischen Landschaft vom 12. bis zum 18. Jahrhundert* (Weimar, 1992).

[107]   L. Enders, 'Die Landgemeinde in Brandenburg. Grundzüge ihrer Funktion und Wirkungsweise vom 13. bis zum 18. Jahrhundert', *Blätter für deutsche Landesgeschichte* 129 (1993), 309–32.

[108]   L. Enders, 'Individuum und Gesellschaft. Bäuerliche Aktionsräume in der frühneuzeitlichen Mark Brandenburg', in J. Peters (ed.), *Gutsherrschaft als soziales Modell* (München, 1995), 155–78.

[109]   L. Enders, 'Das bäuerliche Besitzrecht in der Mark Brandenburg, untersucht am Beispiel der Prignitz vom 13. bis 18. Jahrhundert', in J. Peters (ed.), *Gutsherrschaftsgesellschaften im europäischen Vergleich* (Berlin, 1997), 399–427.

[110]   L. Enders, 'Brandenburg', in J. Klußmann (ed.), *Leibeigenschaft. Bäuerliche Unfreiheit in der frühen Neuzeit* (Cologne, 2003), 40–62.

[111]   L. Enders, 'Grundherrschaft und Gutswirtschaft. Zur Agrarverfassung der frühneuzeitlichen Altmark', *Zeitschrift für Agrargeschichte und Agrarsoziologie* 55 (2007), 95–112.

[112]   S. Göttsch, *"Alle für einen Mann...". Leibeigene und Widerständigkeit in Schleswig-Holstein im 18. Jahrhundert* (Neumünster, 1991).

[113]   W. W. Hagen, 'How mighty the Junkers? Peasant rents and seigneurial profits in sixteenth-century Brandenburg', *Past and Present* 108 (1985), 80–116.

[114]   W. W. Hagen, 'Seventeenth-century crisis in Brandenburg: the Thirty Years' War, the destabilization of serfdom, and the rise of absolutism', *American Historical Review* 94 (1989), 302–35.

[115]   W. W. Hagen, 'Village life in East-Elbian Germany and Poland, 1400–1800: subjection, self-defence, survival', in T. Scott (ed.), *The peasantries of Europe* (London, 1998), 145–89.

[116]   W. W. Hagen, *Ordinary Prussians. Brandenburg Junkers and villagers, 1500–1840* (Cambridge, 2002).

[117]   W. W. Hagen, 'Two ages of seigniorial economy in Brandenburg-Prussia: structural innovations in the 16th century, productivity gains in the 18th century', in P. Janssens and B. Yun Casalilla (eds), *European aristocracies and colonial elites* (Aldershot, 2005), 137–53.

[118]   H. Harnisch, *Die Herrschaft Boitzenburg* (Weimar, 1968).

[119]   H. Harnisch, 'Die Gutsherrschaft in Brandenburg. Ergebnisse und Probleme', *Jahrbuch für Wirtschaftsgeschichte* 4 (1969), 117–47.

[120]   H. Harnisch, 'Bäuerliche Ökonomie und Mentalität unter den Bedingungen der ostelbischen Gutsherrschaft in den letzten Jahrzehnten vor Beginn der Agrarreformen', *Jahrbuch für Wirtschaftsgeschichte* 3 (1989), 87–108.

Bibliography

[121] T. Iida, *Ruppiner Bauernleben 1648–1806. Sozial- und wirtschaftsgeschichtliche Untersuchungen einer ländlichen Gegend Ostelbiens* (Berlin, 2008).

[122] H. Kaak, 'Ländliche Bevölkerung in Brandenburg zwischen Anpassung und Offensive', *Zeitschrift für Agrargeschichte und Agrarsoziologie* 52 (2004), 84–102.

[123] H. Kaak, 'Vom Erbzinsrecht zur Leibeigenschaft – Entstehung agrarischer Zwangsformen im frühneuzeitlichen Brandenburg', *Zeitschrift für Weltgeschichte* 8 (2007), 71–103.

[124] H. Kaak, *Eigenwillige Bauern, ehrgeizige Amtmänner, distanzierte fürstliche Dorfherren. Vermittelte Herrschaft im brandenburgischen Alt-Quilitz im 17. und 18. Jahrhundert* (Berlin, 2010).

[125] J. Klußmann, *Lebenswelten und Identitäten adliger Gutsuntertanen. Das Beispiel des östlichen Schleswig-Holstein im 18. Jahrhundert* (Frankfurt-on-Main, 2002).

[126] J. Klußmann, 'Leibeigenschaft im frühneuzeitlichen Schleswig-Holstein', in J. Klußmann (ed.), *Leibeigenschaft. Bäuerliche Unfreiheit in der frühen Neuzeit* (Cologne, 2003), 213–40.

[127] A. Lubinski, 'Everyday work and manorial culture in Mecklenburg in the 18th and 19th centuries – some problems of research', in K. Sundberg (ed.), *Work and production on manors in the Baltic Sea region 1700–1900* (Stockholm, 2002), 145–64.

[128] F. Mager, *Geschichte des Bauerntums und der Bodenkultur im Lande Mecklenburg* (Berlin, 1955).

[129] H. Maybaum, *Die Entstehung der Gutsherrschaft im nordwestlichen Mecklenburg (Amt Gadebusch und Amt Grevesmühlen)* (Stuttgart, 1926).

[130] H.-H. Müller, *Märkische Landwirtschaft vor den Agrarreformen von 1807* (Potsdam, 1967).

[131] E. Münch, 'Zu den mittelalterlichen Grundlagen der frühneuzeitlichen Adelsgüter Mecklenburgs', *Mecklenburgische Jahrbücher* 112 (1997), 45–60.

[132] E. Münch, 'Mecklenburg und das Problem der Leibeigenschaft Mitte des 16. bis Mitte des 17. Jahrhunderts', in J. Klußmann (ed.), *Leibeigenschaft. Bäuerliche Unfreiheit in der frühen Neuzeit* (Cologne, 2003), 3–19.

[133] J. Nichtweiss, *Das Bauernlegen in Mecklenburg. Eine Untersuchung zur Geschichte der Bauernschaft und der zweiten Leibeigenschaft in Mecklenburg bis zum Beginn des 19. Jahrhunderts* (Berlin, 1954).

[134] M. North, 'Die frühneuzeitliche Gutswirtschaft in Schleswig-Holstein. Forschungsüberblick und Entwicklungsfaktoren', *Blätter für Deutsche Landesgeschichte* 126 (1990), 223–42.

[135] J. Peters, *Märkische Lebenswelten. Gesellschaftsgeschichte der Herrschaft Plattenburg-Wilsnack, Prignitz 1500–1800* (Berlin, 2007).

[136] W. Prange, 'Das adlige Gut in Schleswig-Holstein im 18. Jahrhundert', in C. Degn and D. Lohmeier (eds), *Staatsdienst und Menschlichkeit. Studien zur Adelskultur im späten 18. Jahrhundert in Schleswig-Holstein und Dänemark* (Neumünster, 1980), 56–75.

Bibliography

[137] W. Prange, 'Die Entwicklung der adligen Eigenwirtschaft in Schles
       wig-Holstein', in H. Patze (ed.), *Die Grundherrschaft im späten
       Mittelalter* (Sigmaringen, 1983), 519–53.
[138] C. P. Rasmussen, 'Corvée and paid work. Work and workers at manors
       in Schleswig and Holstein in the 18th century', in K. Sundberg
       (ed.), *Work and production on manors in the Baltic Sea region 1700–1900*
       (Stockholm, 2002), 165–92.
[139] C. P. Rasmussen, 'Ostelbische Gutsherrschaft und nordwestdeutsche
       Freiheit in einem Land – die Güter des Herzogtums Schleswig 1524–
       1770', *Zeitschrift für Agrargeschichte und Agrarsoziologie* 52 (2004), 25–40.
[140] C. P. Rasmussen, 'Innovative feudalism. The development of dairy
       farming and *Koppelwirtschaft* on manors in Schleswig-Holstein in the
       seventeenth and eighteenth centuries', *Agricultural History Review* 58
       (2010), 172–90.
[141] H. Rosenberg, 'The rise of the Junkers in Brandenburg-Prussia
       1410–1653', *American Historical Review* 49 (1943), 1–21, 228–40.
[142] T. Rudert, 'Gutsherrschaft und ländliche Gemeinde. Beobach-
       tungen zum Zusammenhang von gemeindlicher Autonomie und
       Agrarverfassung in der Oberlausitz im 18. Jahrhundert', in J. Peters
       (ed.), *Gutsherrschaft als soziales Modell* (Munich, 1995), 197–218.
[143] T. Rudert, *Gutsherrschaft und Agrarstruktur. Der ländliche Bereich Mecklen-
       burgs am Beginn des 18. Jahrhunderts* (Frankfurt-on-Main, 1995).
[144] R. Schilling, *Schwedisch-Pommern um 1700. Studien zur Agrarstruktur
       eines Territoriums extremer Gutsherrschaft* (Weimar, 1989).
[145] D. Schleinert, *Die Gutswirtschaft im Herzogtum Pommern-Wolgast im 16.
       und frühen 17. Jahrhundert* (Cologne, 2001).
[146] D. Schleinert, 'Personenrechtliche Abhängigkeitsverhältnisse im
       Herzogtum Pommern-Wolgast zwischen Reformation und Dreißig-
       jährigem Krieg', in J. Klußmann (ed.), *Leibeigenschaft. Bäuerliche Unfrei-
       heit in der frühen Neuzeit* (Cologne, 2003), 21–35.
[147] G. Schröder-Lembke, 'Die mecklenburgische Koppelwirtschaft',
       Zeitschrift für Agrargeschichte und Agrarsoziologie 4 (1956), 49–60.
[148] H.-C. Steinborn, *Abgaben und Dienste holsteinischer Bauern im 18.
       Jahrhundert* (Neumünster, 1982).
[149] H. Zückert, 'Vielfalt der Lebensverhältnisse in unmittelbarer
       Nachbarschaft. Die "Gleichzeitigkeit des Ungleichzeitigen" in
       brandenburgischen Dörfern', in J. Peters (ed.), *Gutsherrschaftsgesell-
       schaften im europäischen Vergleich* (Berlin, 1997), 311–21.

Hungary, Slovakia, Balkans

[150] F. Adanır, 'The Ottoman peasantries, c.1360–c.1860', in T. Scott
       (ed.), *The peasantries of Europe* (London, 1998), 268–310.
[151] P. Horváth, *Poddaný l'ud na Slovensku v prvej polovici XVIII. storočia*
       (Bratislava, 1963).
[152] Z. Kirilly, L. Makkai, I. N. Kiss and V. Zimányi, 'Production et
       productivité agricoles en Hongrie a l'époque du féodalisme tardif
       (1550–1850)', *Nouvelles études historiques* 1 (1965), 581–638.

Bibliography

[153] I. N. Kiss, 'Der Agrarcharakter der ungarischen Exporte vom 15. bis 18. Jahrhundert', *Jahrbuch für Wirtschaftsgeschichte* 1 (1978), 147–69.

[154] I. N. Kiss, 'Agricultural and livestock production: wine and oxen. The case of Hungary', in A. Mączak, H. Samsonowicz and P. Burke (eds), *East-Central Europe in transition* (Cambridge, 1985), 84–96.

[155] Z. P. Pach, *Die ungarische Agrarentwicklung im 16.–17. Jahrhundert. Abbiegung vom westeuropäischen Entwicklungsgang* (Budapest, 1964).

[156] A. Špiesz, 'Vývoj agrárnych poměrov v strednej a východnej Európě v novověku a problém existencie druhého nevoľníctva na našom území', *Historický časopis* 15 (1967), 512–58.

[157] D. Ursprung, 'Schollenbindung und Leibeigenschaft: Zur Agrarverfassung der Fürstentümer Walachei und Moldau in komparativer Perspektive (Mitte 16.–Mitte 18. Jahrhundert)', *Südost-Forschungen* 63/64 (2004–05), 124–69.

[158] J. Varga, *Jobbágyrendszer a magyarországi feudalizmus kései századaiban 1556–1767* (Budapest, 1969).

[159] V. Zimányi, *Economy and society in sixteenth and seventeenth century Hungary (1526–1650)* (Budapest, 1987).

Poland

[160] D. Adamczyk, *Zur Stellung Polens im modernen Weltsystem der Frühen Neuzeit* (Hamburg, 2001).

[161] S. Cackowski, *Struktura społeczna i gospodarcza wsi województwa chełmińskiego w okresie pierwszego rozbioru Polski* (Toruń, 1985).

[162] J. Chlebowczyk, *Gospodarka komory cieszyńskiej na przełomie XVII–XVIII w., oraz w pierwszej połowie XVIII w.* (Wrocław, 1966).

[163] R. Czaja, S. Gawlas et al., *Ziemie polskie wobec Zachodu. Studia nad rozwojem średniowiecznej Europy* (Warsaw, 2005).

[164] A. Dunin-Wąsowicz, 'Spatial changes in Poland under the impact of the economic dynamics of the 16th and 17th centuries', in H.-J. Nitz (ed.), *The early-modern world-system in geographical perspective* (Stuttgart, 1993), 172–90.

[165] A. Falniowska-Gradowska, *Świadczenia poddanych na rzecz dworu w królewszczyznach województwa krakowskiego w drugiej połowie XVIII wieku* (Wrocław, 1964).

[166] P. Guzowski, 'A changing economy: models of peasant budgets in fifteenth- and sixteenth-century Poland', *Continuity and Change* 20, 1 (2005), 9–25.

[167] P. Guzowski, *Chłopi i pieniądze na przełomie średniowiecza i czasów nowożytnych* (Cracow, 2008).

[168] R. Heck, *Studia nad położeniem ekonomicznym ludności wiejskiej na Śląsku w XVI. w.* (Wrocław, 1959).

[169] R. C. Hoffmann, *Land, liberties, and lordship in a late medieval countryside. Agrarian structures and change in the Duchy of Wrocław* (Philadelphia, 1989).

Bibliography

[170]   S. Inglot (ed.), *Historia chłopów polskich. Tom I. Do upadku Rzeczypospolitej szlacheckiej* (Warsaw, 1970).

[171]   S. Inglot (ed.), *Historia chłopów sląskich* (Warsaw, 1979).

[172]   A. Kamiński, 'Neo-serfdom in Poland-Lithuania', *Slavic Review* 34 (1975), 253–68.

[173]   A. Kamler, *Chłopi jako pracownicy najemni na wsi małopolskiej w XVI i w pierwszej połowie XVII wieku* (Warsaw, 2005).

[174]   M. Kamler, *Folwark szlachecki w Wielkopolsce w latach 1580–1655* (Warsaw, 1976).

[175]   M. Kanior, *Z badań nad strukturą dochodów wielkiej wlasności. Dobra pomorskie biskupstwa włocławskiego w II. połowie XVIII w.* (Wrocław, 1991).

[176]   J. Kochanowicz, 'The Polish economy and the evolution of dependency', in D. Chirot (ed.), *The origins of backwardness in Eastern Europe. Economics and politics from the Middle Ages until the early twentieth century* (Cambridge, 1989), 92–130.

[177]   J. Leskiewiczowa, *Próba analizy gospodarki dóbr magnackich w Polsce. Dobra wilanowskie na przełomie XVIII/XIX wieku* (Warsaw, 1964).

[178]   A. Mączak, *Gospodarstwo chłopskie na Żulawach Malborskich w początkach XVII wieku* (Warsaw, 1962).

[179]   A. Mączak, 'Export of grain and the problem of distribution of national income in Poland in the years 1550–1650', *Acta Poloniae Historica* 18 (1968), 75–98.

[180]   J. M. Małecki, 'Der Außenhandel und die Spezifik der sozialökonomischen Entwicklung Polens im 16. und 17. Jahrhundert', in M. Biskup and K. Zernack (eds), *Schichtung und Entwicklung der Gesellschaft in Polen und Deutschland im 16. und 17. Jahrhundert* (Wiesbaden, 1983), 21–41.

[181]   J. Muszyńska, *Gospodarstwo chłopskie w starostwie sandomierskim 1510–1663* (Kielce, 1991).

[182]   S. Nawrocki, *Rozwój kapitalizmu w rolnictwe Wielkopolski w latach 1793–1865* (Poznań, 1962).

[183]   M. North, *Die Amtswirtschaften von Osterode und Soltau. Vergleichende Untersuchungen zur Wirtschaft im frühmodernen Staat am Beispiel des Herzogtums Preußen in der zweiten Hälfte des 16. und in der ersten Hälfte des 17. Jahrhunderts* (Berlin, 1982).

[184]   I. Rychlikowa, *Produkcja zbożowa wielkiej wlasności w Małopolsce w latach 1764–1805* (Warsaw, 1967).

[185]   W. A. Serczyk, *Gospodarstwo magnackie w województwie podolskim w drugiej połowie XVIII wieku* (Wrocław, 1965).

[186]   P. Szafran, *Żulawy Gdańskie w XVII wieku* (Gdańsk, 1981).

[187]   Z. Szkurłatowski, *Stosunki spoteczno-ekonomiczne w rolnictwie śląskim w latach 1550–1806 na przykładzie dóbr Luboradz* (Wrocław, 1974).

[188]   M. Topolska, *Dobra szkłowskie na Białorusi wschodniej w XVII i XVIII wieku* (Warsaw, 1969).

[189]   J. Topolski, *Rozwój latyfundium arcibiskupstwa gnieźnieńskiego od XVI do XVIII wieku* (Poznań, 1955).

Bibliography

[190] J. Topolski, 'A model of East-Central European continental commerce in the sixteenth and the first half of the seventeenth century', in A. Mączak, H. Samsonowicz and P. Burke (eds), *East-Central Europe in transition* (Cambridge, 1985), 128–39.

[191] E. Trzyna, *Położenie ludności wiejskiej w królewszczyznach województwa krakowskiego w XVII wieku* (Wrocław, 1963).

[192] B. Wachowiak, *Gospodarka folwarczna w domenach Księstwa Pomorskiego w XVI i na początku XVII wieku* (Warsaw, 2005).

[193] H.-H. Wächter, *Ostpreußische Domänenvorwerke im 16. und 17. Jahrhundert* (Würzburg, 1958).

[194] A. Wawrzyńczyk, *Gospodarstwo chłopskie na Mazowszu w XVI i początkach XVII wieku* (Warsaw, 1962).

[195] A. Wawrzyńczyk, *Gospodarstwo dworskie w dobrach Pabiance 1559–1570* (Wrocław, 1967).

[196] L. Wiatrowski, *Gospodarstwo wiejskie w dobrach pszczyńskich od połowy XVII do początku XIX w.* (Wrocław, 1965).

[197] A. Wyczański, *Studia nad folwarkiem szlacheckim w Polsce w latach 1500–1580* (Warsaw, 1960).

[198] A. Wyczański, 'Tentative estimate of Polish rye trade in the sixteenth century', *Acta Poloniae Historica* 4 (1961), 119–31.

[199] A. Wyczański, *Studia nad gospodarką starostwa korczyńskiego 1500–1660* (Warsaw, 1964).

[200] A. Wyczański, 'The agricultural production and its amount in the XVIth century Poland', *Studia historiae oeconomicae* 4 (1969), 3–13.

[201] A. Wyczański, 'Czy chłopu było źle w Polsce XVI wieku?', *Kwartalnik Historyczny* 85 (1978), 627–41.

[202] K. Zamorski, *Folwark i wieś. Gospodarka dworska i społeczność chłopska Tenczynka w latach 1705–1845* (Wrocław, 1987).

[203] L. Żytkowicz, *Studia nad gospodarstwem wiejskim w dobrach kościelnych XVI w.* (Warsaw, 1962).

[204] L. Żytkowicz, *Studia nad wydajnością gospodarstwa wiejskiego na Mazowszu w XVII wieku* (Warsaw, 1969).

[205] L. Żytkowicz, 'Plony zbóż w Polsce, na Węgrzech i Słowacji w XVI–XVIII w.', *Kwartalnik Historii Kultury Materialnej* 18 (1970), 227–53.

[206] L. Żytkowicz, 'The peasant's farm and the landlord's farm in Poland from the 16th to the middle of the 18th century', *Journal of European Economic History* 1 (1972), 135–54.

[207] L. Żytkowicz, 'Przesłanki i rozwój przytwierdzenia do gleby ludności wiejskie w Polsce – połowa XIV – początek XVI wieku', *Przegląd Historyczny* 75 (1984), 3–22.

Russia

[208] R. Bartlett, 'Serfdom and state power in Imperial Russia', *European History Quarterly* 33 (2003), 29–64.

[209] J. Blum, *Lord and peasant in Russia. From the ninth to the nineteenth century* (Princeton, 1961).

Bibliography

[210]   T. Dennison, *The institutional framework of Russian serfdom* (Cambridge, 2011).
[211]   E. Domar and M. J. Machina, 'On the profitability of Russian serfdom', *Journal of Economic History* 44 (1984), 919–55.
[212]   K. Gestwa, *Proto-Industrialisierung in Rußland. Wirtschaft, Herrschaft und Kultur in Ivanovo und Pavlovo, 1741–1932* (Göttingen, 1999).
[213]   R. Hellie, 'The peasantry', in M. Perrie (ed.), *The Cambridge History of Russia. Vol. 1. From early Rus' to 1689* (Cambridge, 2006), 286–97.
[214]   S. Hoch, *Serfdom and social control in Russia. Petrovskoe, a village in Tambov* (Chicago, 1986).
[215]   S. Hoch, 'The serf economy and the social order in Russia', in M. Bush (ed.), *Serfdom and slavery. Studies in legal bondage* (London, 1996), 311–22.
[216]   A. Kahan, *The plow, the hammer and the knout. An economic history of eighteenth century Russia* (Chicago, 1985).
[217]   I. D. Koval'chenko, *Russkoe krepnostoe krest'ianstvo* (Moscow, 1967).
[218]   J. Kusber, 'Leibeigenschaft in Russland in der Frühen Neuzeit. Aspekte der rechtlichen Lage und der sozialen Praxis', in J. Klußmann (ed.), *Leibeigenschaft. Bäuerliche Unfreiheit in der frühen Neuzeit* (Cologne, 2003), 135–54.
[219]   E. Melton, 'Enlightened seignioralism and its dilemmas in serf Russia, 1750–1830', *Journal of Modern History* 62 (1990), 675–708.
[220]   E. Melton, 'Household economies and communal conflicts on a Russian serf estate, 1800–1817', *Journal of Social History* 26 (1993), 559–85.
[221]   E. Melton, 'The Russian peasantries, 1450–1860', in T. Scott (ed.), *The peasantries of Europe* (London, 1998), 227–66.
[222]   B. N. Mironov, 'Consequences of the price revolution in eighteenth-century Russia', *Economic History Review* 45 (1992), 457–78.
[223]   B. N. Mironov, 'When and why was the Russian peasantry emancipated?', in M. Bush (ed.), *Serfdom and slavery. Studies in legal bondage* (London, 1996), 323–47.
[224]   B. Mironov and B. Eklof, *The social history of Imperial Russia, 1700–1917* (Boulder, 2000).
[225]   D. Moon, *The Russian peasantry 1600–1930. The world the peasants made* (London, 1999).
[226]   A. Stanziani, 'Serfs, slaves or wage earners? The legal status of labour in Russia from a comparative perspective, 17th–19th centuries', *Journal of Global History* 3 (2008), 183–202.
[227]   A. Stanziani, 'The legal status of labour from the seventeenth to the nineteenth century: Russia in a comparative European perspective', *International Review of Social History* 54 (2009), 359–89.

Index

Index

Index

Russia 6, 11, 41
  conflicts between villagers and
    estate officials 35–6
  demesne economy 17, 33
  demesne farming 65, *66*, 105
  grain exports 45
  grain yields *98*, 99
  household wealth of farmers 123
  labour rents 37, 82–3
  marketing of grain by villagers
    113
  mobility restrictions 25, 26
  property rights 30
  rents and taxes 120
  serfdom 17–18
  size of tenant farms 127

Schlagwirtschaft 77, 103, 106
  see also convertible husbandry,
    Koppelwirtschaft
Schleswig(-Holstein), Duchy of 11
  courts and legal system 28
  demesne farming 63, 69, 70, 102,
    103
  expropriation of tenant
    farmers 59–60
  grain yields *98*, 99
  income of tenant farmers and
    impact of rents on 118, 121
  labour rents 78–9
  livestock exports 46
  medieval continuities in demesne
    economy 55
  mobility restrictions 26
  property rights 29, 30
  serfdom 15–16, 22
second serfdom 3, 5, 10–39, 130,
  135
seignorial monopolies *see* monopolies,
  seignorial
serfdom 132
  characteristics of 11–12, 13
  comparison with slave labour 4
  distinction between subjection
    and 12–13, 15, 29
  introduction of as defined by
    law 15–16
  meaning of 11–13

  and property rights 29
  regional realities 13–22
  second *see* second serfdom
Serfdom Act (1781) 14
serfs
  differing opinions of by lords 16
  rights of 12
  stereotypical characteristics of 14
servants 32, 35–6, 37, 72, 78, 79,
  81, 83, 84, 85, 124, 133
  wages for *115*, *116*, 117
service, agricultural 13, 32, 36, 49,
  72–3, 78–85, 119, 120
sheep farming 50, 84, 88
Silesia, Upper, Lower, Duchy of 21,
  42, 45, 48, 71, 77, 88, 91, 101,
  118
  demesne economy 33
  demesne farming 68, 70
  discontinuities in development of
    demesne lordship 53–4
  forced service 72
  grain imports 43
  property rights 29
  serfdom 21
  subjection 21
Slovakia 19, 67, 72, 87, 110 *see also*
  Hungary
smallholders/smallholdings 124,
  126–7, *127*, 128
Smith, Adam
  Wealth of Nations 107
social structure, rural 124–8, 129,
  133
stagnation (agriculture and
  economic) 63, 94, 105, 110,
  122, 129, 133, 135
state interference 41
subjection 20–1, 22–33
  courts and the legal system 28
  distinction between serfdom
    and 12–13, 15
  hereditary 12–13, 15, 19, 20, 28,
    52, 71
  mobility restrictions 22–7
  property rights 29–31
Sweden, Kingdom of 6, 41
  demesne economy 90